AA POCKET GUIDE

LONDON

C0-ASB-674

Written by Susan Grossman
Verified by Christopher Catling
Peace and Quiet section
by Paul Sterry

© The Automobile Association
1997
First published 1990 as *Essential
London*
Revised second edition 1993
Revised third edition 1994
Reprinted 1994; 1995
Revised fourth edition 1997
Reprinted as *Pocket Guide London*
1999
Reprinted 2002

Maps © The Automobile
Association 1997

Ordnance Survey® This product
includes
mapping data licensed from
Ordnance Survey® with the
permission of the Controller of Her
Majesty's Stationery Office.
© Crown copyright 2002. All rights
reserved. Licence number 399221.

Published by AA Publishing, a
trading name of Automobile
Association Developments
Limited, whose registered office
is Millstream, Maidenhead Road,
Windsor, Berkshire SL4 5GD.
Registered number 1878835.

Distributed in the United Kingdom
by AA Publishing, Norfolk House,
Priestley Road, Basingstoke,
Hampshire RG24 9NY.

A CIP catalogue record for this
book is available from the British
Library.

ISBN 0 7495 2123 6

A01332

Colour separation: Mullis Morgan
Ltd, London

Printed by: Printer Trento srl, Italy

Front cover picture: *The Tower* (AA
Photo Library – W Voysey)

Contents

This book employs a simple rating system to help choose which places to visit:

 ✓ 'top ten'

 ◆◆◆ do not miss
◆◆ see if you can
 ◆ worth seeing if you have time

INTRODUCTION

Although London is changing rapidly, with new things to see and do appearing by the day, it is still a city with a profound and lively sense of history. This guide's aim is to provide the sort of information a Londoner would give to a friend visiting the capital. In it you will find everything from the newest museums to a personal selection of shops, hotels and restaurants. What you will not find is information on where to have an Elizabethan banquet; neither are there pages and pages of historical facts. This book does set out to show you a side of the British capital usually reserved for residents!

Present-day London

London had some 16 million visitors last year, over two times its population. For most, first impressions are not particularly inspiring, whether your approach is by train through the dreary south London suburbs from Gatwick, by coach from Heathrow in the west, or by tube into Piccadilly. Once in the city you may be shocked by the crowds, the traffic, the down-and-outs and the homeless teenagers asking for money at the foot of the escalators on the Underground. As for the litter, every year a pile of rubbish big enough to fill Trafalgar Square to five times the height of Nelson's Column is swept up.

Enough of the negatives. Get your bearings and you will discover a city with more green spaces than most, with enough culture to fill a filofax, culinary offerings that span the globe and an exciting future as whole areas of the capital are redeveloped.

Open spaces are an essential part of London's character. They vary from parks so big as to be almost open countryside, to squares little bigger than suburban gardens. This is St James's Square

London looks its best on a Sunday when the streets are quiet (despite the fact that shops are now allowed to open on a Sunday) and the office workers are at home eating roast beef and Yorkshire pudding after a pint in the pub. It looks its best in spring or early summer with the crocuses and daffodils carpeting the parks. And it looks pretty good at night, especially from Waterloo Bridge, with the main monuments lit up along the Embankment.

INTRODUCTION

The Palace of Westminster (universally known as the Houses of Parliament) was rebuilt in the years after 1834, when its predecessor was burnt down. The Victoria Tower dominates this view, with 'Big Ben' looking small in the distance, an illusion which emphasises the huge size of the palace

Old London

Julius Caesar invaded Britain in 55 BC, but it took another 100 years for his legions to land on the south coast and transform this site into a major town. It was Edward the Confessor who moved upstream from the City to establish Westminster, rebuilding the Abbey and the Royal Palace. The City retaliated by electing its own mayor; and it also established itself as the centre for trade, which it still is.

Monarchs came and went. The Black Death of 1348 did not stop the expansion and by the time Henry VIII came to power in 1509, London's population was 50,000. Henry, now famous for having had six wives, sparked off centuries of religious conflict when, in order to divorce his first wife and marry Anne Boleyn, he led the country in a break away from Papal authority. Under the rule of Henry and Anne's

daughter, Elizabeth I, London enjoyed a
flourishing of literature and theatre: this was the
age of Shakespeare and the first Globe theatre,
built in 1599, close to where the new replica
Globe has been built on Bankside. This was also
a time of great debate between Parliament and
monarch over the balance of political power.
The 17th century brought civil war, when
Parliament challenged Charles I's authority.
After the victory of Parliamentarian forces, led
by Oliver Cromwell, Charles was executed and
a period of strict Puritan government ensued.
The monarchy was restored in 1660, when
Charles II ushered in a period of stability,
earning the title of 'Merry Monarch'.
In 1665 yet another plague hit the capital and, a
year later, a small fire in Pudding Lane
triggered off flames that fed the Great Fire of
London which destroyed four-fifths of the city.

Rebuilding was soon under way, and for the next few centuries London prospered. But many of the inhabitants lived in squalor, and crime was rife.

By the 19th century London had expanded enormously, but pockets of the capital were trapped in harsh poverty, vividly described in Charles Dickens' novels.

The first railway appeared during Queen Victoria's reign, as did the first Underground or 'tube' line, which first carried passengers in 1890. From then on suburbs began to spread alongside the railway tracks.

Government

London is the seat of British government, which is a constitutional monarchy. Its laws are made in Parliament, which has two 'Houses', both at Westminster: the House of Commons, where Members are returned by election; and the House of Lords, which can delay and amend

People! On an average day in London you can see bowler-hatted businessmen and penniless paupers, frantically rich yuppies and blue-bloods from the country, the genuinely eccentric and the desperately comic

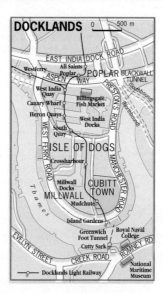

laws but can no longer veto them altogether.
The House of Lords, denounced by some as
unrepresentative and anachronistic, was once
a powerful centre of patronage, and the
creation of peers to add weight to one political
party carried on well into this century. Britain
has no written constitution – a subject of lively
debate. Its form of government evolved
through centuries of power struggles. In theory,
the monarch can still veto the country's laws,
and the Queen must still ratify all statutes. But
this is now a formality which, like the approval
of a new Prime Minister by 'kissing hands', has
become one of the city's political rituals.

New London
They called it the largest building site in the
world as the biggest building boom London
had seen in 25 years got underway. But unless
you base your visit in among the rapidly
developing Docklands or in among the banks
of the City, you would hardly know that some
20 million square feet (1,800,000sq m) of new
office space is being constructed.
Not all Londoners are happy about what's
happening to their city, least of all Prince

Charles, who has complained that post-war architectural clutter has already obscured some of the famous 'views'. Rather late in the day, the Government finally agreed that views along the river and around the Palace of Westminster should be protected. The answer seems to lie in 'groundscrapers', a sort of tower block turned on its side, and they are mushrooming up.

To the east of the city centre, Docklands has already undergone an enormous change as the old warehouses of the West India Dock have been transformed into luxury office buildings and apartments. Of more interest to the visitor is the vast new shopping centre

Hay's Galleria, opposite the Tower of London, with its specialist shops and restaurants. There is just one thing that might hinder Docklands' meteoric rise in status, and that is communications. Inadequate public transport and road links are, however, being improved. In the next few years a massive one-third of the part of London known as the City is being redeveloped in order to place it firmly on the 'global digital highway'. Many new buildings will be offices, but entertainment and culture have not been forgotten. The Broadgate Centre, alongside Liverpool Street station, is dotted with fine sculpture, while at Butler's Wharf, on the south bank of the Thames near

The St Katharine Dock. Originally built in the 1820s, the warehouses here stored wool and wine. They eventually closed in 1968, victims to new downriver ports. Today the expensive boats give a clue to the 'new money' that has transformed the area

Nautical whimsy at Hay's Galleria

Tower Bridge, the Design Museum is devoted to classics of modern design. Here, too, 19th-century warehouses have been turned into shops and up-market restaurants. The thriving London Bridge City complex, with its glass-domed arcade, overlooks the Thames and, just to the west, the Shakespeare Globe Theatre has finally been completed and now offers a unique theatrical experience.

Buildings that went up in the 1960s elsewhere in London are being demolished or getting a facelift. The South Bank (Hayward Gallery, Queen Elizabeth Hall and Royal Festival Hall) and the ugly concrete high-level walkways linking them are getting a massive multi-million pound camouflage. A similarly large amount of money is being spent on turning the old Bankside Power Station into a new showcase for the Tate Gallery's collection of modern art. Whether or not all these changes will enhance the already rather haphazard appearance of London's waterside, only time will tell, but it certainly means that the scene will change.

THE DIFFERENT AREAS

London is split into different areas, each with a distinctive character of its own, from the centre of commerce – the City – to the political world of Westminster. When you are trying to locate an address, the post code can provide useful information. Places in west, west central and southwest London have W, WC and SW respectively after their address, followed by a low number if they are central locations. Addresses with east (E) and east central (EC) after them are in the City, while northwest London (NW) includes areas like Hampstead. The higher the number, the further into the suburbs the location is. London is divided by the River Thames, and most of the action takes place north of it. Stay anywhere in the West End, Knightsbridge, Bayswater or Victoria and you will easily be able to reach the main shopping areas and places of interest.

Inner London

Bayswater

Part of Paddington, near Marble Arch and Hyde Park, Bayswater is full of hotels. The busy Bayswater Road runs past Notting Hill (home of the famous carnival and Portobello Road antique market) and Holland Park to Shepherd's Bush in one direction and along to Marble Arch and Oxford Street in the other. The surrounding streets are quiet, and full of family homes and embassies. Knightsbridge is situated on the other side of Hyde Park.

Hyde Park Corner can be one of London's most unpleasant traffic bottlenecks, but these horses seem quite at home

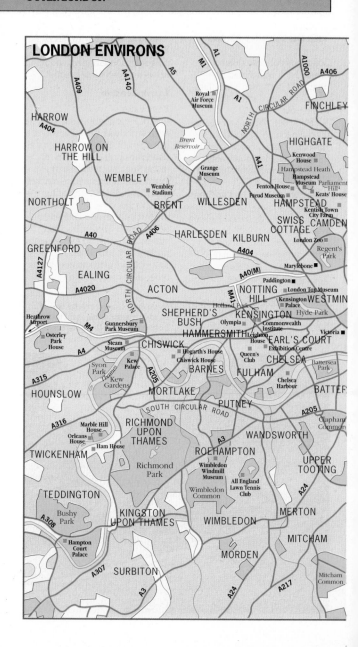

LONDON ENVIRONS

HARROW

HARROW ON THE HILL

WEMBLEY

NORTHOLT

BRENT

WILLESDEN

Royal Air Force Museum

Brent Reservoir

Grange Museum

Wembley Stadium

GREENFORD

EALING

ACTON

HARLESDEN

KILBURN

FINCHLEY

HIGHGATE

Kenwood House

Hampstead Heath

Hampstead Museum

Fenton House

Freud Museum

Parliament Hill

Keats' House

HAMPSTEAD

Kentish Town City Farm

SWISS COTTAGE

CAMDEN

London Zoo

Regent's Park

Marylebone

Paddington

NOTTING HILL

London Toy Museum

Kensington Palace

WESTMIN

Holland Park

KENSINGTON

Hyde Park

SHEPHERD'S BUSH

Olympia

Commonwealth Institute

Leighton House

HAMMERSMITH

EARL'S COURT

Exhibition Centre

Victoria

Queen's Club

CHELSEA

Battersea Park

FULHAM

Chelsea Harbour

BATTER

Heathrow Airport

Osterley Park House

Gunnersbury Park Museum

Steam Museum

CHISWICK

Hogarth's House

Chiswick House

BARNES

Syon Park

Kew Palace

Kew Gardens

Thames

MORTLAKE

PUTNEY

WANDSWORTH

Clapham Common

HOUNSLOW

SOUTH CIRCULAR ROAD

RICHMOND UPON THAMES

Marble Hill House

Orleans House

Ham House

TWICKENHAM

Richmond Park

ROEHAMPTON

Wimbledon Windmill Museum

All England Lawn Tennis Club

Wimbledon Common

UPPER TOOTING

TEDDINGTON

Bushy Park

KINGSTON UPON THAMES

WIMBLEDON

MERTON

Hampton Court Palace

SURBITON

MORDEN

MITCHAM

Mitcham Common

NORTH CIRCULAR ROAD

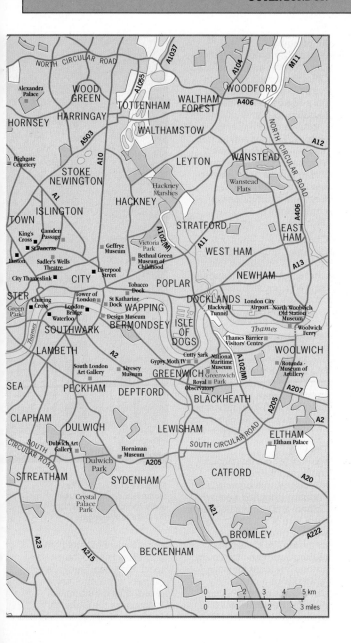

THE DIFFERENT AREAS

Bloomsbury

Bloomsbury is behind New Oxford Street and Tottenham Court Road (with its hi-fi and furniture shops). It includes quiet squares, the British Museum, the University of London and University College Hospital. Famous residents in the 1920s and 1930s were Virginia Woolf, E M Forster, Rupert Brooke, D H Lawrence and Bertrand Russell, all members of the intellectual circle of friends, the 'Bloomsbury Group'.

Chelsea

Chelsea has up-market residential properties, many of them small terraced houses in quiet squares, with fashionable addresses like Cheyne Walk on the river. The new Chelsea Harbour development of restaurants, offices and expensive riverside flats overlooks the boats. The King's Road, the 'mecca' in the 1960s, is still one of London's fashion streets. Chelsea is a tube or bus ride from the West End's shops, a short way from Knightsbridge, and it runs into Kensington.

The City

The City is both the historic capital and the centre of commerce, with boundaries that have extended west into Holborn and east into Docklands. It is a hive of activity during the week as brokers do business on the foreign exchanges, nipping out to one of the many historic hostelries for lunch. At weekends it is relatively quiet, as the owners of the pinstripe suits and the occasional bowler hat desert

The nave of St Paul's. The monument on the left is the overwhelming memorial to the Duke of Wellington

the old Square Mile and head south of the river to the Stockbroker Belt. The younger 'yuppies' with their Porsches relax in a flat in Fulham, the Docklands or the Barbican. Meanwhile, the cockney heart

(cockneys are Londoners born within the sound of Bow Bells) still throbs among the barrows in the East End markets, the historic centre still lives in the ancient Livery Halls, and wigged barristers still administer justice in the peace and inner sanctum of The Temple. The skyline is ever changing, though familiar landmarks like St Paul's Cathedral, the Bank of England and the Old Bailey are still distinguishable through the new towers. It is an area rich in things to see, including 39 city churches and the Museum of London. Close by though not strictly in the City, are the Tower of London, HMS *Belfast*, Tower Bridge, and the Hay's Galleria shopping centre, in the London Bridge City Complex.

THE DIFFERENT AREAS

Covent Garden

A compact central area, next to Soho, immortalised in Shaw's *Pygmalion* where the young Eliza Doolittle sold flowers to the ladies and gents emerging from the Royal Opera House. The Opera House is still there, but the vegetable and flower market moved out in 1974. Today Covent Garden is a magnet for visitors, who throng the cobbled piazza to shop in the central market (idiosyncratic shops selling everything from doll's houses to flower perfumes) and watch the free live street entertainment. At weekends there are crafts and antiques sold from the original wrought-iron trading stands. During the week the open-air cafés, restaurants and wine bars, though few of high quality, are full of film and advertising executives from the surrounding offices. Attractions in the area include the London Transport Museum and several theatres, but there are only a few hotels.

Covent Garden is an essential destination for many shoppers and other visitors

Docklands

Before World War II, London was the greatest port in the world, and 120,000 dockers handled cargoes of spices, furs, rubber and sugar. By the early 1960s the Docks were in irreversible decline and by 1982 everything had closed. Recently, some £2 billion has been invested in the area; Canary Wharf is set to become the new financial centre and hundreds of companies have already moved in, although it will be a while before the developers move out. The Docklands Light Railway, the London City Airport and some 12,000 new homes are already installed, as is a stylish new shopping centre. The best way to see what is happening to Docklands is to travel on the Docklands Light Railway from Bank to Island Gardens on the Isle of Dogs. You can then take the old dockers' subway under the Thames across to Greenwich.

Fulham

Home of the 1980s yuppie brigade – who transformed the streets of this former working class suburbia – Fulham is a mix of seedy tenement houses and fashionable squares. Parts of Fulham are on the river. The Knightsbridge end is up-market, with a good range of restaurants and shopping. Much of the rest is pretty nondescript. Fulham runs into neighbouring Chelsea.

Kensington

The High Street is now largely occupied by chain stores, but this Royal Borough still has its exclusive areas from the antique shops in Kensington Church Street to Kensington Palace (closed during 1996) and the surrounding gardens. Holland Park and the Commonwealth Institute are also in Kensington (see also South Kensington and Earl's Court, page 21).

Knightsbridge

A very central, exclusive location with some of the more expensive hotels and residences in quiet squares. Home of Harrods, Harvey Nichols, Bonham's auctioneers, quality fashion shops in Sloane Street and Knightsbridge, plus numerous galleries and antique shops. Opposite Hyde Park.

Mayfair and Park Lane

High rents render Mayfair, which includes the West End (see page 22), Bond Street and Park Lane, one of the most exclusive areas in London. Famous hotels line one side of Park Lane and overlook Hyde Park, and other well-known hotels like Claridges and the Connaught are near by. Mayfair's village heart is Shepherd Market (home to high-class prostitutes). The area has famous squares like Berkeley and Grosvenor (home of the American Embassy), and includes Bond Street and the *haute couture* fashion houses, as well as Curzon Street's gaming clubs.

Attractions include the Museum of Mankind, near the Burlington Arcade, the Royal Academy, and, in Manchester Square, the Wallace Collection, with its 18th-century paintings and French furniture.

THE DIFFERENT AREAS

Piccadilly and St James's

Piccadilly is a busy thoroughfare connecting Hyde Park and Leicester Square. Green Park runs along one side of it. Within Piccadilly you will find the Ritz Hotel, the Burlington Arcade, the Royal Academy, Fortnum and Mason and airline offices.

St James's, to the south, is a largely male-orientated area with tailors in Jermyn Street, and several gentlemen's clubs. There are theatres in the Haymarket.

Regent's Park

John Nash's beautiful terraces dominate the architecture of Regent's Park, behind the busy Marylebone Road (Madame Tussaud's and the Planetarium) and Baker Street (Sherlock Holmes Museum). Attractions include Queen Mary's Rose Garden, the open-air theatre and the Zoo. The Regent's Canal leads to Camden Lock, with its weekend market, and Little Venice (Maida Vale).

Soho

Soho runs into Covent Garden. Once London's red-light district, Soho has cleaned up its act. Most of the sleazy nightclubs have shut and been replaced by designer restaurants and shops (although the famous Raymond Revuebar Theatre is still going strong). A handful of family-owned businesses still thrive in the area, including Continental delicatessens and patisseries. The Berwick Street market dates back to 1778 (Monday to Saturday 09.00–17.00hrs). One of the few areas of London alive after midnight, with bars, brasseries and discos, Soho includes the cinemas in Leicester Square, the

stores and boutiques of Regent Street and Carnaby Street, the bookshops in Charing Cross Road and cinemas and theatres in Shaftesbury Avenue. Chinatown, south of Shaftesbury Avenue, is also part of Soho.

South Bank

The South Bank Arts Centre across Waterloo Bridge, overlooking the Thames, has for years been the most important landmark for visitors south of the river. It includes

'Little Venice' – the prettiest stretch of the Regent's Canal

the Royal Festival Hall, the National Theatre, the Queen Elizabeth Hall, the Hayward Gallery, the National Film Theatre and the Museum of the Moving Image (MOMI), all due for a £200 million facelift.

South Kensington and Earl's Court

This part of west London is a lively cosmopolitan area, useful to stay in if you are attending an exhibition at Earl's Court or Olympia and near to the main museums (Victoria and Albert, Science, Natural History and Geological) and public transport, but some way from theatres and the West End. It is full of reasonably priced small hotels and guesthouses, though you may find the neighbourhood a bit scruffy. Hotels in or around Kensington High Street are nearer the exclusive shops.

The Strand, Charing Cross

The Strand runs from Trafalgar Square, past Charing Cross Station to the Aldwych which adjoins Fleet Street. To the north is Covent Garden, to the south the river. The Strand's most famous landmark is the Savoy Hotel, and the street contains several theatres. At the Aldwych end are Bush House, the BBC's World Service headquarters, and Somerset House, which now houses the Courtauld Institute Galleries. If you listen to the bells at St Clement Danes Church (on weekdays at 09.00, 12.00, 15.00 or 18.00hrs) you will hear the famous 'Oranges and Lemons' nursery rhyme. London's journalists have largely moved out of Fleet Street to Wapping and the Isle of Dogs, but the barristers are still at the Temple and in the four Inns of Court, a series of secluded cobbled courtyards (you can wander around the quadrangles) seemingly divorced from the hustle and bustle of the rest of London. The Royal Courts of Justice occupy an impressive cathedral-like building in the Strand.

THE DIFFERENT AREAS

Victoria
Numerous small hotels cater for new arrivals whose first view of London is the Station. Busy Victoria Street leads to the Palace of Westminster. Buckingham Palace is to the north, Knightsbridge to the west. It is fairly quiet at night.

West End
The West End is part of Mayfair and Soho, a large area that takes in the shops and department stores in Oxford Street and Regent Street and the theatres around Leicester Square and Covent Garden. North of Oxford Street, Harley Street and Wigmore Street are full of dentists' and doctors' consulting rooms.

Westminster
Seat of Royalty (Buckingham Palace) and Government, Westminster has the Houses of Parliament and Big Ben, Westminster Abbey, Westminster Cathedral, Whitehall and Horse Guards Parade leading up to Trafalgar Square. The area is near the river with good public transport to other parts of the capital. Other sights include the Tate Gallery. A relatively quiet area, especially in the evenings.

Outer London – North

Camden Town
A cosmopolitan residential area somewhat dominated by the crowds who descend at weekends to visit Camden Lock market (see page 80) or to take a boat trip on the Regent's Canal. A short ride by tube into central London. Good shopping for prints, pine furniture and

Buckingham Palace and the Queen Victoria Memorial

books (with many shops open on Sundays). Restaurants (brasseries and Greek) and wine bars, London Zoo, Regent's Park, Little Venice and the villages of Hampstead and Highgate are near by.

Hampstead
On the Northern Line tube into town. Village atmosphere with flats and houses occupied by writers, professionals and bohemians. Narrow pretty streets up behind the station, lots of pubs, restaurants and

boutiques and, at the top of the hill, the wide open spaces of Hampstead Heath. Join the Sunday afternoon kite flyers on Parliament Hill for fine views of the capital. In summer you can swim in the ponds, or watch an open-air concert, while picnicking in the grounds of Kenwood House.

Other Northern Suburbs
Swiss Cottage, down the road from Hampstead, has numerous cosmopolitan restaurants in the Finchley Road and good shopping. Lords, in **St John's Wood**, a short bus ride from Baker Street and near Regent's

Park, will be familiar to cricket fans. Further north is **Highgate** (Karl Marx is buried here) and **Islington**, which has a good antique market on Wednesday and Saturday (Camden Passage) and the Sadler's Wells Theatre.

Outer London – South
It is more difficult to get into central London by public transport from most places south of the river.

Greenwich
Directly across the river from Docklands and the Isle of Dogs via the foot tunnel under the Thames, built in 1897 for

dockers working in the West India Docks. Things to see include the *Cutty Sark*, National Maritime Museum and the Old Royal Observatory. River boats from Greenwich continue along the river to Westminster.

Richmond
Lies between Hampton Court (see **What to See**, page 38) and Hammersmith Bridge. The best way to get there is by boat (summer only) from Westminster Pier. Richmond also encompasses Mortlake, Twickenham, Ham, Barnes, Teddington and Kew (with its magnificent Royal Botanic Gardens). You can walk along the river or stroll through the 2,500 acres of Richmond Park.

Richmond Park is just like 'real' countryside except that the deer don't run away!

Other Southern Suburbs
Dulwich and **Blackheath** are affluent residential areas.

MUSEUMS, EXHIBITIONS AND GALLERIES

WHAT TO SEE

Museums, Exhibitions and Galleries

Among the most popular sights in London are the British Museum, the National Gallery, the Science Museum, Madame Tussaud's, the Tower of London (see page 42) and the Tate Gallery. Three of the major museums, the Science, Natural History and Victoria and Albert, are next to each other in South Kensington, although they are so large you may not find it possible to 'do' more than one or two at a time, and it may be best to stick to one section and 'do' it thoroughly.

Many museums are shut on some, but not necessarily all, public holidays. Most charge admission. Exceptions are indicated in the lists below and include the British Museum, the Tate Gallery, the Bank of England Museum and the National Gallery. Children and senior citizens usually pay less and under-5s nothing. Following is a selection out of the hundreds of museums around the capital.

Central London

◆
BANK OF ENGLAND MUSEUM
Bartholomew Lane, EC2
Opened at the end of 1988, this museum tells the story of the 300 years of history of the 'Old Lady of Threadneedle Street', with an exhibition that includes gold bars, banknotes and a video. Free.
Open: Monday to Friday 10.00–17.00hrs; Sunday and Bank Holidays (summer) 11.00–17.00hrs.
Tube: Bank

BRITISH MUSEUM ✓
Great Russell Street, WC1
One of the biggest and best museums in the world with numerous treasures. Prehistoric Britain, Egyptian mummies, Islamic art, and Greek and Roman antiquities are just a few of the subjects covered. Do not miss the Magna Carta, the Sutton Hoo treasure or the Elgin Marbles. The ethnography collection is in the **Museum of Mankind** in Burlington Gardens. Shop, café and restaurant. Free.
Open: Monday to Saturday 10.00–17.00hrs; Sunday 14.30–18.00hrs.
Tube: Russell Square, Holborn, Tottenham Court Road

◆◆
COURTAULD INSTITUTE GALLERIES
North Block, Somerset House, Strand, WC2
Some of the most exciting French paintings in London are here – with work by Monet, Bonnard, Degas, Seurat and Cézanne. There is also a fine collection of Old Masters. Bookshop and café.
Open: Monday to Saturday 10.00–18.00hrs; Sunday 14.00–18.00hrs.
Tube: Aldwych, Temple, Covent Garden

◆
DESIGN MUSEUM
Butlers Wharf, 28 Shad Thames, SE1
Exhibitions of design and graphics in a modern white building converted from a 1950s warehouse. Magnificent river frontage overlooking Tower Bridge and the City. Run by the

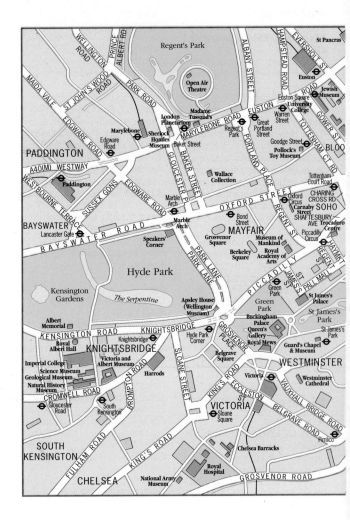

Regent's Park

Open Air Theatre

St Pancras

Euston

Jewish Museum

University College

Euston Square

Warren Street

Great Portland Street

Goodge Street

Pollock's Toy Museum

BLOO

Madame Tussaud's

London Planetarium

Regent's Park

Marylebone

Sherlock Holmes Museum

Baker Street

Edgware Road

Marble Arch

Wallace Collection

Tottenham Court Road

CHARING CROSS RD

Oxford Circus

Carnaby Street

SHAFTESBURY AVE

Trocadero Centre

SOHO

Piccadilly Circus

PADDINGTON

Paddington

A40(M) WESTWAY

WESTBOURNE TERRACE

SUSSEX GDNS

EDGWARE ROAD

GLOUCESTER PL

Marble Arch

OXFORD STREET

Bond Street

MAYFAIR

Museum of Mankind

Royal Academy of Arts

REGENT ST

BAYSWATER

Lancaster Gate

BAYSWATER ROAD

Speakers' Corner

Grosvenor Square

Berkeley Square

Kensington Gardens

Hyde Park

The Serpentine

PARK LANE

PARK LANE

Apsley House (Wellington Museum)

PICCADILLY

Green Park

Green Park

St James's

PALL MALL

St James's Palace

St James's Park

St James's Park

Albert Memorial

Royal Albert Hall

KENSINGTON ROAD

Knightsbridge

KNIGHTSBRIDGE

Hyde Park Corner

GROSVENOR PLACE

Buckingham Palace

Queen's Gallery

Royal Mews

Guard's Chapel & Museum

WESTMINSTER

Imperial College

Science Museum

Geological Museum

Natural History Museum

CROMWELL ROAD

Victoria and Albert Museum

BROMPTON ROAD

Harrods

SLOANE STREET

Belgrave Square

KING'S ROAD

Victoria

ECCLESTON ST

Westminster Cathedral

VAUXHALL BRIDGE ROAD

Gloucester Road

South Kensington

VICTORIA

Sloane Square

BELGRAVE ROAD

Pimlico

SOUTH KENSINGTON

FULHAM ROAD

KING'S ROAD

Chelsea Barracks

CHELSEA

National Army Museum

Royal Hospital

GROSVENOR ROAD

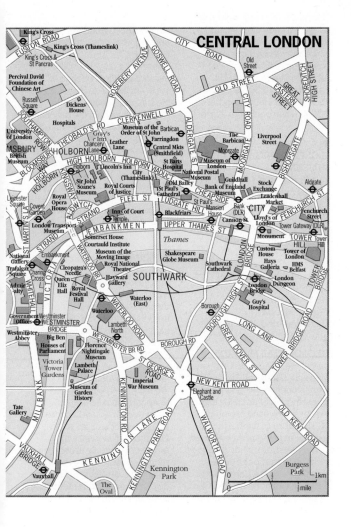

CENTRAL LONDON

King's Cross
EUSTON ROAD
King's Cross (Thameslink)
King's Cross &
St Pancras
CITY ROAD
Old Street
GREAT EASTERN STREET
SHOREDITCH HIGH STREET
Percival David
Foundation of
Chinese Art
Russell
Square
Dickens'
House
GOSWELL ROAD
ROSEBERY AVENUE
OLD STREET
CITY ROAD
Hospitals
CLERKENWELL RD
Liverpool
Street
University
of London
SOUTHAMPTON ROW
THEOBALD'S RD
Museum of the
Order of St John
Gray's
Inn
Farringdon
ALDERGATE ST
The
Barbican
Barbican
MOORGATE
BISHOPSGATE
MSBURY
British
Museum
BLOOMSBURY WAY
HOLBORN
Chancery
Lane
Leather
Lane
Central Mkts
(Smithfield)
Museum of
London
Moorgate
Stock
Exchange
Aldgate
HIGH HOLBORN
HOLBORN
HOLBORN VIADUCT
St Barts
Hospital
National Postal
Museum
Guildhall
HIGH HOLBORN
Holborn
Lincoln's Inn
KINGSWAY
Sir John
Soane's
Museum
City
(Thameslink)
Old Bailey
St Paul's
Cathedral
Bank of England
Museum
Leadenhall
Street
Leicester
Square
Royal
Opera
House
Covent
Garden
Royal Courts
of Justice
FLEET ST
LUDGATE HILL
CHEAPSIDE
St Paul's
Mansion
House
Bank
(DLR)
CITY
Lloyd's of
London
Leadenhall
Market
FENCHURCH ST
Fenchurch
Street
ST MARTIN'S LA
STRAND
ALDWYCH
Inns of Court
Temple
Blackfriars
Cannon St
UPPER THAMES ST
Tower Gateway (DLR)
Monument
TOWER HILL
Tower
Hill
London Transport
Museum
STRAND
EMBANKMENT
Somerset House
Courtauld Institute
Thames
Custom
House
Tower of
London
National
Gallery
Embankment
Museum of the
Moving Image
Royal National
Theatre
Hayward
Gallery
Shakespeare
Globe Museum
Southwark
Cathedral
Hays
Galleria
HMS
Belfast
TOWER BRIDGE
Trafalgar
Square
Charing
Cross
WATERLOO BR
Cleopatra's
Needle
Queen
Eliz
Hall
SOUTHWARK
London
Dungeon
Admir
alty
WHITEHALL
Royal
Festival
Hall
Waterloo
(East)
LONDON BRIDGE
London
Bridge
Government
Offices
VICTORIA
WESTMINSTER
Waterloo
Borough
Guy's
Hospital
Westminster
Abbey
WESTMINSTER
BRIDGE
Big Ben
Houses of
Parliament
WATERLOO ROAD
Lambeth
North
WESTMINSTER BR RD
BOROUGH RD
BOROUGH HIGH ST
GREAT DOVER ST
LONG LANE
TOWER BRIDGE ROAD
Victoria
Tower
Gardens
Florence
Nightingale
Museum
Lambeth
Palace
ST GEORGE'S ROAD
Museum of
Garden
History
Imperial
War Museum
NEW KENT ROAD
Elephant and
Castle
OLD KENT ROAD
Tate
Gallery
MILLBANK
KENNINGTON RD
KENNINGTON LANE
KENNINGTON PARK ROAD
WALWORTH ROAD
VAUXHALL
BRIDGE
KENNINGTON LANE
Kennington
Park
Burgess
Park
Vauxhall
The
Oval
0   1km
0   mile

MUSEUMS, EXHIBITIONS AND GALLERIES

Conran Foundation, established by Sir Terence Conran, and modelled on the Boilerhouse which they leased out in the basement of the Victoria and Albert Museum until 1986.
Open: daily, 10.30–17.30hrs.
Tube: Tower Hill or London Bridge (riverboat from Tower Pier)

◆
FLORENCE NIGHTINGALE MUSEUM
2 Lambeth Palace Road, SE1
A small museum dedicated to the life of the Lady of the Lamp, next to St Thomas's Hospital where she founded the first School of Nursing in 1860. Unique collection, includes the medicine chest and lamp she used during the Crimean War.
Open: Tuesday to Sunday 10.00–16.00hrs.
Closed: Monday.
Tube: Waterloo, Westminster

◆
GEOLOGICAL MUSEUM
part of the Natural History Museum, Cromwell Road, SW7
Gem stones, rocks and fossils, an earthquake simulator and a video of a volcano are all part of 'The Story of the Earth' exhibition in the newly opened Earth Galleries. Other exhibits include 'Britain before Man', 'Treasures of the Earth', and 'Britain's Offshore Oil and Gas'. Combined ticket with Natural History Museum.
Open: Monday to Saturday 10.00–17.50hrs; Sunday 11.00–17.50hrs. Free admission 16.30–18.00hrs (Monday to Friday); 17.00–17.50hrs (weekends and Bank Holidays).
Tube: South Kensington

◆
HAYWARD GALLERY
South Bank Centre, Belvedere Road, SE1
Housed in a purpose-built, modern building, opened in 1968. On the South Bank (next to the National Theatre and the Royal Festival Hall) the gallery has no permanent collection, but it is an important venue for major exhibitions concentrating on the work of 20th-century artists.
Open: daily, 10.00–18.00hrs (Tuesday and Wednesday until 20.00hrs).
Closed: between exhibitions.
Tube: Waterloo

◆◆
IMPERIAL WAR MUSEUM
Lambeth Road, SE1
This newly redesigned museum, with exhibits never previously displayed, tells the story of war from Flanders to the Gulf in a triple height exhibition hall with exhibits including aircraft, Polaris missiles and torpedoes. The building which houses the museum, formerly the original 'Bedlam', Bethlehem Royal Hospital (a lunatic asylum), has been revamped and adapted to include such features as an enormous glazed atrium. Aircraft seem to fly around the room and visitors can roam among the displays. Interactive displays and various themes including the 'Blitz' and 'Trench Experiences' and the 'Post War World'. The museum features a major art collection too, with harrowing works by modern artists. Free after 16.30hrs daily.
Open: daily, 10.00–18.00hrs.
Tube: Lambeth North, Elephant and Castle

MUSEUMS, EXHIBITIONS AND GALLERIES

Quiet recreation – inside the London Brass Rubbing Centre

◆
LEIGHTON HOUSE
12 Holland Park Road, W14
This gorgeous time-warp house contains many paintings by pre-Raphaelite artists such as Millais, Watts, Burne-Jones and Alma-Tadema, all friends of the painter and sculptor Lord Leighton whose house this was from the 1860s. The studio used by Leighton now hosts concerts and exhibitions. Free.
Open: Monday to Saturday 11.00–17.30hrs.
Closed: Sunday.
Tube: High Street Kensington

◆
LONDON BRASS RUBBING CENTRE
St Martin-in-the-Fields Church, Trafalgar Square, WC2
Brass rub to medieval music. Seventy replica church brasses to choose from. Charge. (NB You can also rub brasses at Westminster Abbey – Monday to Saturday 09.00–17.00hrs.)
Open: Monday to Saturday 10.00–18.00hrs; Sunday 12.00–18.00hrs.
Tube: Charing Cross, Leicester Square

◆
LONDON DUNGEON
28–34 Tooley Street, SE1
Opposite Hay's Galleria and near HMS *Belfast*. Gruesome, dimly lit exhibition of medieval history including the Plague, the Great Fire of London, Theatre of the Guillotine, astrology and witchcraft. Lots of torture and noises. Life-size reconstruction of Pudding Lane. No under-10s on their own.
Open: daily, 10.00–18.30hrs (17.30hrs October to March).
Tube: London Bridge

MUSEUMS, EXHIBITIONS AND GALLERIES

◆◆
LONDON PLANETARIUM
Marylebone Road, NW1
Combined ticket with Madame
Tussaud's. Spectacular views of
the heavens with shows every
40 minutes. The Astronomers
exhibition includes wax figures
such as Einstein and Galileo
and three-dimensional images
of their discoveries. For times of
shows tel: 0171 486 1121.
Tube: Baker Street

◆◆
LONDON TRANSPORT MUSEUM
The Piazza, Covent Garden, WC2
All sorts of transport from trolley
buses to trains housed in the
old Flower Market building in
the Covent Garden piazza. Lots
of things to scramble over, and
you can work signals on trains
or 'drive' a bus or a tube train.
Special events for children and
families in the school holidays.
Open: daily, 10.00–18.00hrs
(last entry 17.15hrs).
Tube: Covent Garden

◆◆
MADAME TUSSAUD'S
Marylebone Road, NW1
One of London's most popular
attractions (long queues) with
life-like wax figures (updated
continuously) of famous people
including historical figures, film
stars, sportsmen and pop stars,
plus the Chamber of Horrors,
with its reconstructions of some
grisly and historic crimes.
Combined ticket with the
Planetarium (see above).
Open: Monday to Friday 10.00–
17.30hrs; Saturday and Sunday
09.30–17.30hrs.
Tube: Baker Street

◆◆
MUSEUM OF LONDON
150 London Wall, EC2
The Museum if you are
interested in the history of
London and Londoners. Open-
plan galleries display exhibits,
beginning with prehistoric cave
people and moving on to
reconstructions of Roman
London, including Londinium's
triumphal arch and a wealthy
Roman merchant's house. Also
exhibited is an art deco lift from
Selfridges department store,

the Lord Mayor's State Coach, reconstructed Victorian shops, a 1930s Ford motorcar, an air-raid shelter and a reconstruction of Newgate gaol. One of the highlights is a short re-enactment of the Fire of London. Café. Free after 16.30hrs.
Open: Tuesday to Saturday 10.00–17.50hrs; Sunday 14.00–17.50hrs.
Closed: Mondays, except Bank Holidays.
Tube: Barbican, St Paul's, Moorgate

◆◆
MUSEUM OF THE MOVING IMAGE (MOMI)
South Bank Centre, SE1
The largest museum in the world devoted to cinema and television, tracing the history of film from the Chinese Shadow Plays of 2000 BC to the latest in optical technology. Watch yourself fly over London, appear in a TV chat show, or

The National Gallery's collections are superb

act in a cowboy film. Shop.
Open: daily, 10.00–18.00hrs.
Tube: Waterloo, Embankment

♦♦♦
NATIONAL GALLERY ✓

Trafalgar Square, WC2
One of the world's finest
collections of western European
paintings from about 1250 to
1900. The information sheet
*A Quick Visit to the National
Gallery* highlights 16
masterpieces; and there are
quiz sheets for children during
the school holidays. The new
Sainsbury Wing, with its extra
gallery space, also has a shop
and a restaurant. Free.
Open: Monday to Saturday
10.00–18.00hrs; Sunday 14.00–
18.00hrs. Wednesdays in July
and August open until 20.00hrs.
Tube: Charing Cross, Leicester
Square

♦♦
NATIONAL PORTRAIT
GALLERY
St Martin's Place, WC2
Around 9,000 portraits,
arranged chronologically, of
famous Britons from the Middle
Ages to Princess Diana. Free
(charge for some exhibitions).
Open: Monday to Saturday
10.00–18.00hrs; Sunday
noon–18.00hrs.
Tube: Charing Cross, Leicester
Square

♦♦♦
NATURAL HISTORY
MUSEUM ✓

*Cromwell Road, South
Kensington, SW7*
Unstuffy museum whose most

popular exhibits are the huge
dinosaur skeletons and the
frighteningly realistic tableau of
carnivorous dinosaurs that
move and roar. 'Creepy
Crawly' exhibition, videos and
an exciting interactive human
biology hall. Combined
entrance ticket with the
Geological Museum (see page
28).
Open: Monday to Saturday
10.00–17.50hrs; Sunday 11.00–

*The Natural History Museum –
superb Victorian architecture*

17.50hrs. Free admission after
16.30hrs (Monday to Friday)
and 17.00hrs (weekends).
Tube: South Kensington

◆
QUEEN'S GALLERY
Buckingham Palace, SW1
A rare chance to see works of
art from the Royal Collection,
in a former Palace chapel.

Open: (when an exhibition is
being held) Tuesday to Saturday
10.00–17.00hrs; Sunday 14.00–
17.00hrs.
Tube: Victoria

◆
ROCK CIRCUS
London Pavilion, Piccadilly, W1
An audio animatronic spectacular
on two floors with models of the
immortals of rock and pop from
Buddy Holly to Michael Jackson,
plus instruments, authentic
settings, spectacular lighting
and sound effects. Revolving
stage shows.
Open: daily, 11.00–21.00hrs
(from noon Tuesday; until
22.00hrs Friday and Saturday).
Extended hours in summer.
Tube: Piccadilly Circus

◆◆
ROYAL ACADEMY OF ARTS
Burlington House, Piccadilly, W1
The home of the Fine Art Society,
founded in 1768. Changing
exhibitions and famous annual
Summer Exhibition (June to
August) where you can buy the
work of some 1,000 artists. Shop.
Open: daily, 10.00–18.00hrs.
Tube: Piccadilly Circus, Green
Park

◆◆◆
SCIENCE MUSEUM ✓

*Exhibition Road, South
Kensington, SW7*
One of the most exciting
museums for children. Original
press-button Children's Gallery
in the basement plus hi-tech
'Launch Pad' on the first floor.
Measure your heartbeat or star
in your own video. Also Space
Gallery, medical history, gallery

MUSEUMS, EXHIBITIONS AND GALLERIES

of aeroplanes, films and scientific instruments.
Open: Monday to Saturday 10.00–18.00hrs; Sunday 11.00–18.00hrs.
Tube: South Kensington

◆
SHERLOCK HOLMES MUSEUM
221b Baker Street
The famous address of super-sleuth Sherlock Holmes and his friend Dr Watson. The museum has maintained its Victorian

atmosphere, and includes a range of exhibits from the published adventures of Mr Holmes. Shop.
Open: daily, 09.30–18.00hrs.
Tube: Baker Street

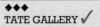

◆◆◆
TATE GALLERY ✓

Millbank, SW1
The national collection of British art plus 20th-century paintings and sculpture, works by Turner

in the Clore Gallery, modern prints and changing exhibitions. Free except for exhibitions. Lunchtime restaurant (closed Sundays) and coffee shop.
Open: Monday to Saturday 10.00–17.50hrs; Sunday 14.00–17.50hrs.
Tube: Pimlico

In 1871 the **Cutty Sark** *beat the world record by sailing from China to England in 107 days. She is now moored at Greenwich*

♦♦♦
VICTORIA AND ALBERT MUSEUM (V&A)

South Kensington, SW7; entrances in Cromwell and Exhibition Roads
An outstanding museum of European and Oriental fine and decorative art and design, tracing the history of glass, furniture and jewellery, textiles and dress, from early Christian times to the present. Exhibitions from around the world, with miles of galleries. Also here is a national collection of watercolours, sculpture and Constables, plus exhibitions. Restaurant. Donations.
Open: Monday 12.00–17.50hrs; Tuesday to Sunday 10.00–17.50hrs.
Tube: South Kensington

Forest Hill

♦
HORNIMAN MUSEUM AND GARDENS
London Road, Forest Hill, SE23
An art nouveau museum with a curious mix of exhibits, from stuffed birds to tribal masks. Also musical instruments and aquarium.There is a park with nature trail and good views of London. Exhibitions, lectures, and concerts. Café. Free.
Open: Monday to Saturday 10.30–17.30hrs; Sunday 14.00–17.30hrs.
British Rail: Forest Hill (1½ miles east of Dulwich)

Greenwich

♦
CUTTY SARK AND GIPSY MOTH IV
Greenwich Pier, SE10
Two ships moored on the Thames at Greenwich. In 1869 the *Cutty*

MUSEUMS, EXHIBITIONS AND GALLERIES

The Freud Museum

Sark was used to transport
Chinese tea and wool from
Australia and was the fastest
vessel afloat. Below decks, an
exhibition explains her history.
The *Gipsy Moth IV* was the boat
used by Francis Chichester on
the first single-handed voyage
around the world in 1966/7.
Open: Cutty Sark: April to
September, Monday to Saturday
10.00–18.00hrs; Sunday 12.00–
18.00hrs (closes 17.00hrs rest of
year). *Gipsy Moth*: April to
September, Monday to Friday
10.00–13.00hrs and 14.00–
18.00hrs; Saturday 10.00–
18.00hrs; Sunday 12.00–
18.00hrs (17.00hrs October).
Closed: November to March.
British Rail: Cannon Street,
Waterloo East, Charing Cross
and London Bridge to Maze Hill
or Greenwich

◆
NATIONAL MARITIME MUSEUM
Romney Road, Greenwich, SE10
A wonderful museum, devoted to British seafaring, partly housed in England's first Palladian-style house, designed by Inigo Jones. Navigation room with instruments, contemporary ship models, paintings, barges and galleries devoted to Lord Nelson and Captain Cook.
Open: March to October, Monday to Saturday 12.00–18.00hrs; Sunday 14.00–18.00hrs. November to February, Monday to Saturday 10.00–17.00hrs; Sunday 14.00–17.00hrs.
British Rail: see previous entry

Hampstead

◆
FENTON HOUSE
Windmill Hill, Hampstead Grove, Hampstead, NW3
A William and Mary house built in 1693, with a collection of early musical instruments and porcelain and furniture.
Open: April to October, Saturday, Sunday and Bank Holidays 11.00–17.30hrs; Monday to Wednesday 13.00–17.30hrs; also March, weekends 14.00–18.00hrs.
Tube: Hampstead

◆
FREUD MUSEUM
20 Maresfield Gardens, Hampstead, NW3
The imposing red-brick home of Sigmund Freud is now a small museum and research institute containing his furniture, including the famous couch, books and collection of antiquities.

Open: Wednesday to Sunday 12.00–17.00hrs.
Closed: Monday and Tuesday.
Tube: Finchley Road

◆
KEATS' HOUSE
Keats Grove, Hampstead, NW3
The Regency house where Keats lived and wrote from 1818 to 1820. Furniture of the period, his bedroom, plus cabinets of letters, manuscripts and relics relating to his friends and family, and the pretty garden in which he wrote *Ode to a Nightingale*. Keats' lover and nurse, Fanny Brawne, lived in the house next door. Voluntary donation.
Open: Monday to Friday 14.00–18.00hrs; Saturday 10.00–17.00hrs; Sunday 14.00–17.00hrs.
Tube: Hampstead

◆◆
KENWOOD HOUSE (THE IVEAGH BEQUEST)
Hampstead Lane, Hampstead, NW3
A beautiful Robert Adam mansion overlooking the Heath, with weekend open-air lakeside jazz and symphony concerts. Lord Iveagh gave the mansion and his collection of paintings to the nation in 1927. Magnificent English 18th-century paintings, a Rembrandt self-portrait and Vermeer's *Lady Playing the Guitar*. Free. Restaurant, café.
Open: April to September, 10.00–18.00hrs (16.00hrs October to March).
Tube: Walk across the Heath from Hampstead tube; or take the 210 bus from Archway or Golders Green

MUSEUMS, EXHIBITIONS AND GALLERIES

Hampton Court – Richmond-on-Thames

**◆◆◆
HAMPTON COURT PALACE** ✓

East Molesey, Surrey
Bought by Cardinal Wolsey in 1514, this 1,000-roomed palace is richly furnished with tapestries, and heavily panelled with gilded ceilings. It was enlarged by Henry VIII, who built the Great Hall, and again altered by Wren in 1689. Opulent state rooms, tapestries and famous paintings. Set in magnificent formal gardens.
Open: Monday 10.15–18.00hrs; Tuesday to Sunday 09.30–18.00hrs (16.30 in winter). Gardens open dawn to half an hour before dusk.
British Rail: Hampton Court (also river trips from Westminster Pier, Richmond and Kingston)

Twickenham

◆
MARBLE HILL HOUSE
Richmond Road, Twickenham
Palladian villa built in the 18th century as a summer residence for George II's mistress, Henrietta Howard. Gilded carvings and oil paintings. Landscaped gardens sweeping down to the Thames with concerts on Sunday evenings in July and August. Free.
Open: April to October, daily, 10.00–18.00hrs; November to March, Wednesday to Sunday 10.00–16.00hrs.
British Rail: Waterloo to St Margaret's; or river launches in summer from Westminster Pier to Richmond, then by bus

The entrance to Hampton Court Palace, flanked by heraldic 'King's Beasts'

Landmarks, Cathedrals and Monuments

HMS *BELFAST*
Morgan's Lane, off Tooley Street, SE1
Huge Royal Navy cruiser from World War II. Admire it from the river or clamber over the seven decks to see the gun turrets and galleys.
Open: daily, mid-March to October 10.00–18.00hrs (17.00hrs rest of year).
Tube: Tower Hill, Monument or London Bridge; Tower Gateway (Docklands Light Railway) or ferry from Tower Pier

◆◆
BIG BEN
Clock Tower, Palace of Westminster, SW1
Most probably named after Sir Benjamin Hall, who commissioned the enormous bell and completed work on the 316 feet (96m) tower in 1859. To climb the tower you must be in a group, be aged over 11 and have a letter of permission from your MP or embassy.
Tube: Westminster

◆◆◆
BUCKINGHAM PALACE
The Mall, SW1
The Queen's residence; she is at home when the Royal Standard is flying. You can only go in during August and September, or if invited to a State banquet or a garden party. But you can watch the Changing of the Guard at 11.30hrs from early April to mid-August daily and in winter on alternate days, which is free.
Open: Palace: daily, 7 August to 28 September 09.30–17.30hrs

Completed in 1882, the Law Courts are a superb example of Victorian Gothic architecture

(last admission 16.30hrs).
Tube: Victoria, St James's Park, Green Park

◆◆◆
HOUSES OF PARLIAMENT
St Margaret Street, SW1
The Palace of Westminster includes the House of Commons and the House of Lords. You can visit the Strangers' Gallery while the House is sitting; queue outside St Stephen's entrance. Call the Public Information Office (tel: 0171 219 4272) for details. Free.
Tube: Westminster

LAW COURTS
Strand, WC2
The Royal Courts of Justice date from 1874. Watch from the public

galleries in 60 courts. Free.
Open to visitors: weekday
sessions, 10.00–13.00hrs and
14.00–16.00hrs.
Tube: Temple, Aldwych

◆
LLOYD'S OF LONDON
1 Lime Street, EC3
International insurance market
housed in an eye-catching,
modern, rocket-like building
designed by Richard Rogers.
Closed to the public because of
terrorist bomb threats, but
worth viewing from the outside,
especially when lit up by
coloured spotlights at night.
Tube: Bank, Monument, Aldgate

◆
MONUMENT
Monument Street, EC3
Fluted, hollow Doric column
built by Sir Christopher Wren to
commemorate the Great Fire of
London. The view from the
platform, just below the golden
urn (311 steps up), used to
stretch right across the Thames
and City but is now somewhat
obscured by office blocks.
Open: April to September,
Monday to Friday 09.00–
18.00hrs; Saturday and Sunday
14.00–18.00hrs; October to
March, Monday to Saturday
only 09.00–16.00hrs.
Tube: Monument

◆
OLD BAILEY
Newgate Street, EC4
Central Criminal Court.
Open: Public Gallery: Monday
to Friday 10.15–13.00hrs and
13.45–16.00hrs when court is
sitting.
Closed: weekends and August.
Tube: St Paul's

*Construction of the huge Thames
Barrier began in 1974*

◆◆◆
ST PAUL'S CATHEDRAL ✓

Ludgate Hill, EC4
Largest and most famous church
in the City, the fourth or fifth on
the site, built by Sir Christopher
Wren. Burial place of Nelson
and the Duke of Wellington.
Splendid interior views from the
Whispering Gallery. Climb over
600 steps up to the dome for
spectacular views. Guided tours
(except Sundays). Free, but
donations requested. A charge
is made for the crypt, galleries
and dome.

Open: Monday to Saturday
08.30–16.15hrs; Sunday:
services.
Tube: St Paul's

◆
SOUTHWARK CATHEDRAL
London Bridge, SE1
A fine Gothic building with the
Harvard Chapel dedicated to
the founder of Harvard
University. Burial place of
Shakespeare's brother. Free.
Open: daily, 08.00–18.00hrs.
Tube: London Bridge

◆
10 DOWNING STREET
Off Whitehall, SW1
The official residence of the
Prime Minister; the Chancellor
of the Exchequer lives next
door at No 11. The buildings
themselves have unpretentious
Georgian façades. The world-
famous street has a barrier at
the end so you cannot get close.
Tube: Westminster, Charing
Cross

◆◆
THAMES BARRIER
Unity Way, Woolwich SE18
Between the Blackwall Tunnel
and the Woolwich Ferry. The
world's largest movable flood
barrier stretching 1,700 feet
(520m) across the Thames. It
consists of 10 steel gates which,
when raised, stand as high as a
five-storey building, as wide as

the opening in Tower Bridge and weigh more than a Naval destroyer. Visitors' centre.
Open: Monday to Friday 10.30–17.00hrs; Saturday, Sunday and Bank Holidays 10.30–17.30hrs.
British Rail: Charlton Station (then 15 mins walk); or river boat (1hr 15 mins from central London, 25 mins from Greenwich)

◆◆◆
TOWER BRIDGE
Tower Bridge, SE1
Opened in 1894, it took eight years to build. Splendid views from the walkway across the top of the towers (lift). The Tower Bridge Experience tells the story of the bridge's history. Visit the Victorian engine rooms with the original steam pumps. The huge bascules are raised to let big ships through.
Open: April to October, daily 10.00–18.30hrs; November to March, daily 09.30–18.00hrs.
Tube: Tower Hill, London Bridge

◆◆◆
TOWER OF LONDON ✓
Tower Hill, EC3
William I's Tower, built on a vantage point on the river to defend the city from invaders. Its chequered past has included a prison (for the likes of Guy Fawkes and Sir Walter Raleigh), the Royal Mint and the Royal Observatory. Now the home of the Crown Jewels. The Keep is one of the earliest fortifications in western Europe. Galleries of armour and torture instruments. Yeoman Warders (popularly known as Beefeaters) wear Tudor uniform. The nightly 700-year-old Ceremony of the Keys can be watched only by written

application to the Resident Governor, Queen's House, HM Tower of London, EC3N 4AB.
Open: March to October, Monday to Saturday 09.00–18.00hrs; Sunday 10.00–18.00hrs; November to February, Monday to Saturday 09.00–17.00hrs; Sunday 10.00–17.00hrs.
Tube: Tower Gateway, or Tower Hill (Docklands Light Railway)

◆◆◆
WESTMINSTER ABBEY
Parliament Square, SW1
Famous kings and queens crowned and buried in the vaults, including Elizabeth I. Coronation Chair, Poet's Corner and the Stone of Scone (due to be returned to Scotland in the near future) are also here.
Open: Nave and cloisters (free), Sunday between services, weekdays 08.00–18.00hrs (19.45 Wednesday). Royal Chapels (charge). Monday to Friday 09.00–16.45hrs; Saturday 09.45–14.45hrs and 15.45–17.45hrs. Also visit the Chapter House, Pyx Chamber, Abbey Museum and College Gardens.
Tube: St James Park, Westminster

◆◆
WESTMINSTER CATHEDRAL
Ashley Place, SW1
Behind Victoria Street. England's largest and most important Roman Catholic Church. Fine marble and mosaics. Free. Take a lift to the top of the 273-foot (83m) campanile (charge).
Open: bell tower: mid-March to October 09.00–17.00hrs; cathedral: daily, 07.00–20.00hrs (19.00hrs in winter).
Tube: Victoria

Tower Bridge is beautiful at any time of day or night

Parks, Gardens and Cemeteries

Few cities in the world can boast as many parks and open spaces, from the acres of Royal Parks, originally the hunting grounds of the Royal Palaces, to tiny grassed-over squares, a haven from the bustle of London.

Central London

◆

HOLLAND PARK

Behind Kensington High Street, a pleasant, almost suburban park, with many nannies pushing perambulators. Orangery with changing exhibitions, open-air theatre and summer concerts.
Tube: Holland Park, High Street Kensington

PARKS, GARDENS AND CEMETERIES

◆◆
HYDE PARK

Once a hunting forest belonging to Henry VIII. Wide open spaces characterise Hyde Park, which is enclosed by Bayswater, Knightsbridge and Park Lane, and has the Serpentine Lake at its centre. It is the largest of the central London parks and is home to a surprisingly large range of birds. Hire a horse to ride down Rotten Row, take out a boat, swim if you can brave the British weather, or listen to the soapbox orators at Speaker's Corner.
Tube: Hyde Park Corner, Marble Arch

◆◆◆
KENSINGTON GARDENS

Merges with Hyde Park at the bridge over the Serpentine. The formal gardens of Kensington Palace. Do not miss the statue of Peter Pan, the Albert Memorial (currently under restoration, but visitor centre open), the Round Pond, or the Orangery.
Tube: High Street Kensington, Queensway

◆◆◆
REGENT'S PARK

The park with the most to offer: the Zoo, the open-air theatre

A detail from the Albert Memorial

PARKS, GARDENS AND CEMETERIES

(Shakespeare), a boating lake and swings for children, rowing boats for adults, cafés and Queen Mary's splendid rose garden. Alongside the park runs the Outer Circle, which is lined with elegant, columned Nash terraces.

Tube: Baker Street (Regent's Park, Camden Town for Zoo)

◆
ST JAMES'S PARK
The oldest of the Royal Parks with a lake and good views of Buckingham Palace. Alongside the Mall it joins up with Green Park, which runs along Piccadilly. Once a favourite retreat of Charles II.

Tube: Green Park, St James's Park

Outer London

◆◆
GREENWICH PARK
Overlooking the Thames with the Old Royal Observatory, original home of Greenwich Mean Time, on the crest of the ridge, and the National Maritime Museum at the bottom. This is one of the most historic of the Royal Parks, laid out by Le Nôtre for Charles II in 1662. There is a hollow oak, reputedly danced around by Elizabeth I, the deer enclosure, a boating pool and a playground.

Tube: Docklands Light Railway from Bank to Island Gardens, then subway under the Thames; or British Rail from Charing Cross, Waterloo East, London Bridge and Cannon Street (weekdays only) to Maze Hill or Greenwich; or river boats from Westminster, Charing Cross and Tower Piers

◆
HAMPSTEAD HEATH
High open space in north London, with splendid views from Jack Straw's Castle pub and Parliament Hill, which is popular with kite flyers, Sunday afternoon walkers, dogs and joggers. Bank holiday fairground. Playground and bathing ponds. Wooded walk to Kenwood House (see page 37) where there are lakeside concerts on summer weekend evenings.

Tube: Hampstead, Belsize Park

◆
HIGHGATE CEMETERY
Swain's Lane, N6
Last resting place of, among others, Karl Marx. Western side by guided tour only (weekends on the hour, 10.00–16.00hrs, and summer weekdays at noon, 14.00 and 15.00hrs). Photos only with permit.

Open: Eastern side, April to September, daily 10.00–17.00hrs; rest of year until 16.00hrs.

Tube: Archway; or bus 210, C11, 143, 271

◆◆◆
KEW GARDENS (ROYAL BOTANIC GARDENS)
World-famous Royal Botanic Gardens, south of the river, with plant houses: alpines, palms, and a tropical conservatory. Splendid trees and flowering shrubs – there are over 44,000 different species – line grand vistas. You can have tea in the Orangery. Kew Palace is furnished in George III style.

Open: daily, 09.30–dusk.

Tube: Kew Gardens; or British Rail to Kew Bridge; or buses 65, 27. Boats depart from Westminster Pier (summer)

Red deer stag – imposing resident of Richmond Park

◆
RICHMOND PARK
In southwest London, 2,500 acres (1,000ha) used as a hunting ground by Charles I, with deer, ancient oak trees and ponds. Horses for hire, riverside walks, cycle tracks and several magnificent residences.
Tube/British Rail: Richmond

◆
SYON PARK GARDENS
In Brentford, Middlesex. Fifty-five acres (22ha) of gardens that include a lake, rose garden, butterfly house, vintage cars, Great Conservatory and sculptures. The 16th-century house, which was remodelled by Robert Adam, is the London residence of the Duke of Northumberland.
Open: House: April to September, Wednesday to Sunday and Bank Holidays 11.00–17.00hrs (Sunday only in October). Gardens: all year, daily 10.00–18.00hrs (17.00hrs in winter); Butterfly House: daily, 10.00–17.00hrs and Heritage Motor Museum 10.00–17.30hrs.
Tube: Gunnersbury; then bus 237 or 267 to Brent Lea Gate

PEACE AND QUIET

Wildlife and Countryside in and around London by Paul Sterry

At first glance, the centre of London, like many other capitals, may not seem the most suitable place to observe wildlife: house sparrows, starlings and pigeons are often the only creatures to be seen. However, visit the right locations or travel as little as 30 miles (48km) from the centre and a fascinating array of plants and animals can be discovered. Even the central Royal Parks, such as St James's Park and Hyde Park, have squirrels and woodpigeons, and the presence of tame birds on their lakes lures wild birds into these rather unnatural settings. The same is true of London Zoo, set in Regent's Park; sometimes it is difficult to tell the captive creatures from the wild ones. Examples of most habitats typical of southern England lie within a day's journey of the capital. The remains of once great hunting forests can be found at Windsor and Epping and freshwater habitats from lakes to rivers abound, many being associated with the course of the Thames, which bisects the city. Even specialised and wildlife-rich habitats such as heathland and chalk grassland lie close to the city and are well worth a visit.

The Royal Parks of Central London

In the heart of the capital, the Royal Parks provide a haven of comparative solitude. The vegetation of these parks is almost entirely dictated by man and the wildlife often exotic and introduced, but the presence of animals which are tolerant of humans often draws in more appealing wild species.

St James's Park is home to ubiquitous house sparrows which are bold enough to feed from people's hands, and flocks of feral pigeons come and go from nearby Trafalgar Square. A surprising resident of both this park and nearby Hyde Park is the woodpigeon. It is not persecuted here as it is in the rest of Britain and consequently has become extremely confiding. Both St James's Park and Hyde Park contain lakes and ponds and, of these, the Serpentine is the most interesting, winding its way along the northern side of Hyde Park.

To explore the Serpentine, park on the northern shore just off The Ring, near Serpentine Bridge. Walk around the edge of the water and around the Long Water as well. Look for moorhens and coots among the tufted ducks, mallards and Canada geese. Grey herons are sometimes seen early in the morning and great crested grebes nest on the island near the Boat House. In spring, pairs of grebes perform elaborate displays on the water prior to mating and nest building.

Small patches of woodland in Hyde Park and adjoining Kensington Gardens sometimes harbour migrant birds such as spotted flycatchers, redstarts and willow warblers in spring, while jays are resident throughout the year. They will

PEACE AND QUIET

often come and investigate those visitors who seem a likely source of food, often with bold grey squirrels in hot pursuit. These charming animals were introduced from North America, but have adapted extremely well to British woodlands and urban environments. Grey squirrels are fascinating creatures to watch as they dextrously use their paws to eat, but be careful not to get too close because they can, and do, bite if provoked.

Richmond Park

Lying just south of the Thames in west London, Richmond Park is the most 'natural' and largest of the London Royal Parks and without doubt the one which holds the most wildlife interest. Famous for its deer, which are numerous and obligingly tame, the park is an enclave of attractive, rolling countryside set among the sprawling suburbs, and is popular with Londoners and visitors alike. Richmond Park has ponds, open grassland with scattered trees and areas of more mature woodland. Rhododendron thickets provide a wonderful flowering display in June which attracts the admiration of both visitors and pollinating insects. Insects are not confined to the flowers, however, and a careful search of the foliage may reveal the amazingly colourful rhododendron leafhopper, as well as oak bush crickets and speckled bush crickets. Despite the houses and tower blocks which surround and almost overlook the park, the

birdlife is surprisingly rich. Kestrels can be seen hovering over the grassland on the look-out for voles, and spotted flycatchers, great spotted woodpeckers, tits, nuthatches and treecreepers can all be found in the wooded areas. The ponds also attract some interesting wildfowl and reed warblers have been known to attempt to nest around their margins.

Richmond Park's Deer
As soon as you enter the park, you cannot fail to notice the deer. Sizeable herds of both red and fallow deer roam the grassland, and because they are forever confined within its boundaries, they are easily seen throughout the year.
In the autumn, the red deer in particular are at their most spectacular: dominant stags with huge sets of antlers gather together their harems of hinds, and bellow warnings at other males. Visit the park on a cold October morning and you will be treated to the memorable sound of stags 'belling', their breath steaming in the damp air, and the sight of crashing antlers as rivals do battle.
For good views of the deer, park in designated spots at Robin Hood Gate and walk towards Pen Ponds. They are usually close to the road and are easiest to see on the north side where the grassland is more open. However, the lusher vegetation to the south provides a more appropriate setting. If you find a young deer in spring, leave it alone: otherwise the mother may desert.

Windsor Great Park and Virginia Water

Despite its popularity, Windsor Great Park, which lies to the west of London, is still a fine example of mature English parkland. The landscape is dotted with stately trees and, nestling within its woodlands, the tranquil surface of Virginia Water reflects its leafy surroundings like a mirror. Throughout the park, ancient oaks with gnarled and twisted

One of the ancient oaks in Windsor Great Park

trunks and withered looking branches play host to large numbers of insects, including several rare species of beetles not known elsewhere in the country. During July and August, purple hairstreak butterflies flit among the foliage, while at ground level, speckled woods and small tortoiseshells are common.

If you are lucky, you might see a purple hairstreak butterfly in Windsor Great Park

The birds also benefit from the variety and age of the trees. Diminutive lesser spotted woodpeckers feed unobtrusively throughout the park, while green and great spotted woodpeckers are conspicuous and noisy, making them easier to locate. Kestrels hunt over the open ground and, during the summer months, hobbies are occasionally seen as they scythe through the air in search of swallows and house martins.

For a lovely circular walk, park either in the large car park beside the A30 or in the car park beside the A329 at Blacknest. From the shores of the lake Canada geese and ducks can be seen; this is the best place in England to see mandarin ducks. Carp, tench and other fish can be seen spawning from the bridges in the early summer.

During the winter months, this variety of birds is sometimes joined by small numbers of winter visitors such as scaup, goldeneye and smew. These are particularly easy to see as the water begins to freeze because the birds become concentrated as the area of open water reduces.

Hawfinch
The woodlands around Virginia Water are renowned for being one of the most reliable places in the counties around London to see hawfinches. Normally rather shy and elusive birds, hawfinches are frequently found in the vicinity of hornbeam trees close to the car park, and their massive, seed-cracking bills give them an unmistakable silhouette when perched high in a tree. Hawfinches are generally easiest to see during the winter months when the leaves are off the trees. In flight, they show a lot of white on the wings and tail.

The Surrey Heaths
Lying to the southwest of London, the landscape of Surrey varies from mature woodland to chalk grassland. Above all, however, it is the open heathland for which the county is best known and, despite being so close to the capital, there are still areas, such as Chobham Common, which have escaped housing development. The heathers (from which the habitat gets its name) and the gorse are the glory of the heathlands and,

from June to August, turn the landscape into seas of yellows and purples.

Although heathlands may look natural, their appearance is actually due to generations of tree clearance by man. The resulting nutrient-poor, acidic soils have an extremely specialised flora, with ling, bell heather, cross-leaved heath and gorse predominating, interspersed with tussocks of the characteristic purple moorgrass. In wetter areas, beautiful yellow spikes of bog asphodel grow among the carpet of *Sphagnum* moss, and carnivorous sundew plants digest insects caught on their sticky leaves.

Heathlands are renowned for their spiders, misty autumn mornings highlighting the tell-tale webs and strands of silk with dew. Insects also abound and colourful emperor moths are on the wing in March and April, while July and August are the months for grayling and silver-studded blue butterflies and numerous species of dragonfly and damselfly. Among the low vegetation, mottled grasshoppers hop to safety and bog bush crickets clamber among the cross-leaved heath. The insect life supports a variety of birds, with stonechats and pipits being particularly conspicuous. Among the larger clumps of gorse, the more secretive Dartford warbler, long since extinct in its place of discovery in Kent, scolds intruders into its territory.

Emperor moths are big and spectacular and not uncommon on heathlands in spring

PEACE AND QUIET

Although they prefer the cover of vegetation, during March and April, males often perch on the tops of gorse spikes, singing for all they are worth.

To visit Chobham Common, park in one of the car parks off the Chobham Road (B383) near Chertsey. Thursley Common is another fine example of southern heathland. Park on the west side of the common, which lies between Farnham and Haslemere, off the A287. Headley Heath has a car park to the west of the B2033 near Leatherhead.

Reservoirs

Vast quantities of water are consumed by Londoners. To quench this thirst, numerous reservoirs have been built around the outskirts of the city, these benefiting not only the human population but also large numbers of birds. These in turn lure birdwatchers, who find the variety of species and numbers of birds rivals many rural areas. Most notable and easily accessible of the reservoirs is Staines, situated under the flight path of many of the jets which leave Heathrow. Although the noise may detract from some people's enjoyment, it certainly seems to do little to upset the birds, who carry on feeding regardless. From the central causeway which separates the two halves of the reservoir, huge numbers of ducks can be seen during the winter months.

If the water is very low, green sandpipers might stop off to feed in muddy reservoir bottoms

> **Mediterranean Gull**
> Search through the thousands of black-headed gulls which are found on London's lakes and playing fields and you may be lucky enough to find a Mediterranean gull during the winter months.
> Despite its name, the Mediterranean gull is turning up with increasing regularity in the region. Adults in winter have a blood-red bill, dark 'eyelid' markings and pure white wings.

From March to May, Staines Reservoir is a good spot to watch for passage migrants such as sand martins, swallows, swifts and black terns. Rarities such as white-winged black terns and whiskered terns appear occasionally and the list of unusual birds is not confined to water-loving species.

Every now and then, the water authorities have to drain one or other of the reservoirs in order to remove the build-up of silt.

This rich expanse of mud, teeming with small invertebrates, attracts waders such as dunlins and redshanks. To visit Staines Reservoir, park in one of the residential roads off Town Lane – this heads north from the A30 to the west of the reservoir – and walk to the causeway. Brent Reservoir is another good spot to visit. It lies near the junction of the North Circular Road and Edgware Road in West Hendon. Park off Church Lane.

The North Downs and Box Hill

Within easy reach of London, the North Downs, a long ridge of chalk running east to west through Surrey, provides fabulous views over rolling English countryside. The North Downs Way provides long-distance walks, but for those with less time to spare, the wildlife and scenery of Box Hill Country Park near Dorking is particularly rewarding. Although the park suffers a lot from public pressure, the range of plants and animals within its boundaries is immense. Centuries of woodland clearance and sheep grazing have combined to produce the close-cropped grassland so typical of chalky soils. On this land, known as 'downland', constant nibbling by sheep and rabbits has encouraged a rich diversity of flowering plants which would otherwise be crowded out by the grasses. During the summer months, yellow rattle, marjoram, thyme, sainfoin, kidney vetch and knapweeds provide a

Yellow rattle – a showy plant of downland in early summer

kaleidoscope of colour, and attract insects such as hoverflies, burnet moths, and butterflies including silver-spotted skipper, common blue and chalkhill blue.

In southern England, orchids are the real botanical speciality of chalk downland, with many colourful and extraordinary species being found around Box Hill. Purple spikes of fragrant orchids and the aptly named pyramidal orchid grow alongside the diminutive greenish-yellow plants of musk orchids while, where the scrub provides a degree of shade,

PEACE AND QUIET

common twayblades and man orchids can sometimes be found. Many of the downland invertebrates are also unique to the chalky soils, and snails are often abundant, the calcium providing building materials for their shells. Humbug-like shells of white-lipped and brown-lipped snails are conspicuous, while immense edible snails, introduced to Britain by the Romans, are best seen on damp days among the scrub.

On many slopes on the North Downs, scrub and woodland still persist. Box Hill gains its name from the box tress which predominate in some areas, but elder and yew are also common. To find Box Hill Country Park car park, follow signs from the A24 just to the north of Dorking or from the A25 between Dorking and Reigate. Other superb areas of downland can be found at Ranmore Common. The car park is located on the minor road which runs from Dorking to East Horsley. The area is particularly well known for the wide range of butterflies that can be found during spring and summer.

The Thames Estuary

On its journey from London to the North Sea, the Thames fans out to form an extensive estuary bordered on the north by Essex and on the south by Kent. Although at times bleak and forbidding, and often industrialised, this habitat is the winter home to thousands of birds and a nursery ground for many commercially important species of fish. Access to the marshes is often difficult, but at

Two-Tree Island near Southend in Essex and from Cliffe to High Halstow in Kent good views of the mudflats and their teeming birdlife can be had.

Much of coastal Kent and Essex is protected from floods and gales by sea walls, and to the naturalist both the landward and the seaward sides are of interest. Inland, the coastal marshes are grazed by cattle and are breeding grounds for redshank, snipe and yellow wagtail in the summer, while in the winter, short-eared owls and hen harriers hunt for small mammals. Hen harriers are graceful birds of prey that feed by quartering the ground. Both sexes have a conspicuous white rump. The plumage of the male is grey while that of the female is brown. The vast areas of mud and silt which the Thames has deposited over the centuries become exposed at low tide and provide a rich feeding ground for birds. Shelduck dabble in the shallow water for small molluscs, while brent geese, visitors from Arctic Russia, alternate between feeding grounds in the creeks and the close-cropped fields behind the sea walls. Huge numbers of dunlin, knot, grey plover, redshank, curlew and godwit probe the mud for lugworms and molluscs, taking to the wing in tight flocks at the slightest disturbance.

Northward Hill is an RSPB reserve which protects part of the north Kent marshes as well as oak woodland. It lies northeast of Rochester and can be reached on Northwood Road from High Halstow village. Grey herons and nightingales breed

Marshes such as this one in Kent are excellent for birds

here and long-eared owls are seen in winter.

On the Isle of Sheppey is Elmley, another RSPB reserve. A signposted track heads east from the A249, one mile (2km) north of Kingsferry Bridge. There are grazing marshes and freshwater scrapes here which attract large numbers of waders and wildfowl, especially during the winter.

Epping Forest

Only a short distance from the centre of London, Epping Forest is an extensive area of ancient woodland with wide forest rides. Sadly, it no longer harbours the deer which once provided sport for kings, the disturbance caused by increased public pressure having driven them away. The decline in tree management has also had an adverse effect on the diversity of the forest's wildlife, especially its birds and mammals. Despite this, however, Epping Forest still has magnificent trees and is a wonderful escape from the city for both the casual stroller and those more interested in observing the plant and animal life of the woodland.

PEACE AND QUIET

Epping Forest. It is difficult to believe that this great tract of ancient woodland is right on London's doorstep

During the winter months, flocks of redpolls, occasionally joined by small numbers of siskins, feed among the high branches of the trees. The flocks often form loose associations with blue tits, coal tits, long-tailed tits and goldcrests, whose high-pitched calls attract the attention of the observer. Since the trees lack leaves at this time of year,

The Beech Tree
Stately beech trees are common in Epping Forest. This magnificent tree was planted both as a boundary marker and for its wood; it does, of course, also occur naturally in the region. The timber not only makes excellent firewood but is also popular among carpenters, being particularly good for turning.
Beech is also spectacularly colourful in spring with its bright green leaves and in autumn when they turn a beautiful, golden brown.

and its long history of association with man. The area with the most wildlife interest is in Great Monk Wood. Woodland birds, butterflies and fungi are numerous.

The Thames

Although its role in the life of the city has dwindled over the centuries, the Thames is still a focal point and has much to offer the visitor. Beyond Docklands, the river opens out to form the vast Thames Estuary which is the haunt of thousands of wintering birds, while up-river towards Henley it gradually becomes more attractive as waterside vegetation and lush agricultural land appear along its banks. Once so polluted that no life survived in the waters that flowed through London, the Thames is now undergoing a slow process of being cleaned up and fish are beginning to recolonise.

A variety of birds can also be seen along the rivers' course in central London, the most conspicuous being black-headed gulls, which are present for most of the year except the height of summer. Flocks of these noisy birds often include herring gulls or even common gulls, all of which commute between the Thames and London's many reservoirs and parkland lakes.

As the banks of the Thames become more rural, kingfishers occasionally fly by in a dazzling flash of blue and red, and you may also be treated to the breathtaking sight of a flight of graceful mute swans.

following the movements of the birds is comparatively easy. The buds burst into leaf in April and May just as many migrant birds are arriving from Africa. Whitethroats, blackcaps and willow warblers are common spring songsters, and colourful redstarts flit amongst the dappled branches.

Epping Forest lies northwest of Loughton. There are several car parks to be found on the minor roads through the forest. The Conservation Centre at High Beach provides information about the Forest

PEACE AND QUIET

Mute Swan

On some of London's lakes and on the Thames away from central London, mute swans are a familiar sight. These stately birds are considered property of the Crown and have benefited from the protection this has provided. In the spring, large nests of twigs and grasses are built among the riverside vegetation and are fiercely guarded by the male bird, which is known as a cob. Mute swans are so-called because they are generally silent. In flight, however, their wings produce a throbbing sound.

Along the course of the Thames from Wraysbury near Heathrow to Reading, there is a mosaic of hundreds of gravel pits.

To explore this network around Wraysbury, take the minor road around Horton, Wraysbury, Datchet and Hythe End to the west of the M25. There are extensive gravel pit workings around Theale, near Reading. Try also Burghfield and Sheffield Bottom.

Where these gravel pits have not yet filled with water, they provide the ideal conditions for one of Britain's scarcest breeding waders. Little-ringed plovers lay their camouflaged eggs on the pebbly ground and are inconspicuous as they quietly incubate them.

Freshwater Habitats

Less than 25 miles (40km) north of central London, the valleys of the rivers Chess and Lea offer a rich variety of natural freshwater habitats which contrast markedly with the formal appearance of the ponds and lakes in the city's parks.

The River Chess is an attractive, shallow river between Rickmansworth and Chorley which has rich waterside vegetation. Metallic-blue damselflies and mayflies dance around the bushes and family parties of mute swans paddle up and down, in places such as Chenies becoming quite tame. Patches of thick vegetation sometimes harbour breeding sedge warblers and overhanging branches serve as perches for colourful kingfishers. During the winter, small numbers of green sandpipers, easily recognised in flight by their white rumps, feed along the river margins. They also frequent the margins of gravel pits and man-made lakes such as Stocker's Lake near Rickmansworth.

Further east, the Lea Valley also holds interesting freshwater habitats. The RSPB's reserve at Rye House Marsh near Hoddesdon has a public birdwatching hide overlooking an interesting area of marsh. Both reed and sedge warblers sing from the cover of the reeds during May and June while common terns, which breed on man-made rafts in the reserve's pools, scream overhead. During migration time, swallows, martins and black terns pass through the area and a wide selection of waders such as green and common sandpipers, redshank, ruff and little-ringed plovers put in brief appearances. During the winter months, the reserve is frequented by good numbers of wildfowl, gulls and waders, such as snipe and jack snipe. Rye House Marsh lies to the east of Hoddesdon in Hertfordshire and there is a car park opposite Rye House railway station. The Old River Lea is another good wetland area and is especially rich in dragonflies. It can be reached by crossing footbridges from Waltham Abbey in Hertfordshire. There are numerous gravel pits to the north of nearby Cheshunt.

Water rail – retiring inhabitant of marshes and watersides

Kew Gardens

An entrance fee allows access to the world-famous Royal Botanic Gardens at Kew, which have been open to the public since 1841. To anyone interested in botany, the gardens are a paradise, containing plants from all over the world, and with over 30,000 species and varieties of plant on display, Kew provides an endless source of interest. Flowers are grown both outdoors and indoors within elaborate showpiece greenhouses, so there is plenty to see all year round. Spring, however, is especially colourful with blooms of every conceivable hue on show.

PEACE AND QUIET

In contrast to the wonderful displays of flowers in the formal borders and those in the botanical study areas, part of the garden has been devoted to a more natural setting and was originally laid out by Capability Brown. Here the visitor can stroll through attractive, lakeside woodland, the ground carpeted with flowers early in the year, and be serenaded by woodland birds. Because they are not persecuted, many species have become remarkably confiding, and jays and woodpigeons in particular seem to have little fear of people.

Kew Gardens. As well as the various glasshouses, there are 300 acres (120ha) of grounds to explore here

FOOD AND DRINK

Restaurants
Restaurants with the best food in the capital are generally pricey, especially in the evening. But there are exceptions and at lunchtime many offer the chance to try a fixed-price menu at a fraction of the evening price. A selection of outstanding restaurants, renowned for their chefs and the quality of their *haute cuisine*, is given here.

Alastair Little, 49 Frith Street, W1 (tel: 0171 734 5183). A small, but stylish, street-level, café-like restaurant, with bare black tables and a daily changing menu that roams Europe and further afield. Reasonably expensive. Closed Saturday lunchtimes and Sundays.

Bibendum, Michelin House (First Floor), 81 Fulham Road, SW3 (tel: 0171 581 5817). First-floor, elegant, fashionable restaurant full of animated celebrities, with chef Simon Hopkinson rejecting *nouvelle cuisine* in favour of regional, usually classic French, though fish and chips or rice pudding may be on the changing menu at lunchtime. Open daily.

Chez Nico at Ninety Park Lane, Grosvenor House Hotel, 90 Park Lane, W1 (tel: 0171 409 1290). Nico Ladenis has exchanged his own restaurant for this up-market hotel patronised by expense account diners (though lunch can be very good value). Simply one of the best restaurants in London. Expensive. Closed Saturday lunch and Sunday.

M Bibendum oversees his restaurant

Connaught, Carlos Place, W1 (tel: 0171 499 7070). Chef Michael Bourdin has now been at the Connaught for 20 years and in many other respects, little seems to have changed here despite the passage of time: impeccable waiters serve classic French dishes to pillars of the establishment in the wood-panelled and club-like restaurant. Open daily.

The Four Seasons, Four Seasons Hotel, Park Lane, W1 (tel: 0171 499 0888 ext 3172). Fine views of Hyde Park add to the inventiveness of Jean-Christophe Novelli's classic cooking. Rather expensive, but Novelli is tipped as the chef of the 1990s.

FOOD AND DRINK

Le Gavroche, 43 Upper Brook Street, W1 (tel: 0171 408 0881). Owned by the famous Roux brothers, with Albert Roux's son, Michel, now in charge of the kitchen. Serious French restaurant with an impressive menu taking in both simple dishes and elaborate creations. Closed weekends.

The Ivy, 1 West Street, WC2 (tel: 0171 836 4751). Haunt of the famous and arty, decorated with murals by Howard Hodgkin and Patrick Caulfield, a relaxed restaurant offering a good range of traditional and unusual dishes, strong on fish. Mid-range prices. Open daily.

The Oak Room, Le Meridien Hotel, 21 Piccadilly, W1 (tel: 0171 734 8000). A rather grand, gilt and mirrored, baroque banqueting hall with an international feel and a rather loud pianist, offering *cuisine creative, traditionelle* or *gourmand* and changing specialities. Expensive, but good-value set dinner. Closed Saturday lunch and Sundays.

Quaglino's, 16 Bury Street, SW1 (tel: 0171 930 6767). Sir Terence Conran's vast 468-seat restaurant in St James's was greeted with scepticism when it opened in 1993 but has since been hailed as London's best new restaurant, a stylish place serving faultless and imaginative food, to the sound of a pianist (weekdays) or jazz trio (weekends). Open daily.

The Restaurant, Hyde Park Hotel, 66 Knightsbridge (tel: 0171 259 5380). Marco Pierre White has moved on from his original restaurant (Harvey's in Wandsworth) to this grand

Exterior style reflects the interior qualities of La Tante Claire

address where White's flair is evident in dishes that are both classic and daring. Closed Saturday lunch and Sunday.

Le Soufflé, Inter-Continental Hotel, 1 Hamilton Place, W1 (tel: 0171 409 3131). Arguably the best hotel food in London. A small, tastefully decorated dining room, where chef Peter Kromberg specialises in imaginative soufflés as well as outstanding French dishes. Closed Saturday lunch, Sunday evening and Monday.

La Tante Claire, 68 Royal Hospital Road, SW3 (tel: 0171 351 0227). Pierre Koffman is at the helm of this small temple of French gastronomy offering high standards and good-value lunches, otherwise very expensive. Closed weekends.

The following is a mixed bag of restaurants (also see separate sections for **Vegetarian** and **Ethnic**) selected for their better than average food, ambience and value for money.

Expensive:
In Hotels
The colonial style restaurant in the **Lanesborough**, on Hyde Park Corner (tel: 0171 259 5599) and the **Savoy's** Grill Room, The Strand (tel: 0171 836 4343), favourite of businessmen, are both very expensive. The long-awaited, lavishly restored and refurbished **Dorchester** in Park Lane (tel: 0171 629 8888) has a new Oriental restaurant to complement the Grill and Terrace. The Chelsea Room in the **Hyatt Carlton Tower**, 2 Cadogan Place (tel: 0171 235 1234) near Harrods is a good choice for lunch (including wine); or try the club-like, wood-panelled Rib Room which

FOOD AND DRINK

specialises in roast meat and shellfish. The family-run **Goring** in Grosvenor Gardens (tel: 0171 396 9000) has fixed-price menus offering traditional dishes prepared imaginatively by chef John Elliott. The Causerie at **Claridge's** in Brook Street, W1 (tel: 0171 629 8860) is much loved by Royalty who come for the comfortable, elegant setting and the wonderful *smörgåsbord* lunch. The restaurant also offers early evening buffets (from 17.30hrs).

With Dancing

The **Savoy's** opulent River Restaurant (tel: 0171 836 4343) overlooks the Thames and has a band most nights. There is also dancing (on Saturdays) in the sumptuous Louis XVI style French baroque dining room at

Tea at the Ritz – you will need to book if you want a table at this famous establishment

FOOD AND DRINK

the **Ritz** (tel: 0171 493 8181) and big-band dancing in the Ritz's Palm Court (where they serve afternoon teas) on Friday and Saturday nights.

Reasonable:
The Brackenbury, 129 Brackenbury Road, W6 (tel: 0181 748 0107). Charming wine bar restaurant serving delicious, simple cuisine. Friendly service, interesting wine list. Closed Saturday and Monday lunchtimes and Sunday evenings.
Le Caprice, Arlington House, Arlington Street, SW1 (tel: 0171 629 2239). Chic, black and white brasserie with a large menu, in the heart of Mayfair, which attracts celebrities, especially for Sunday brunch. Open every day until midnight.
Chez Moi, 1 Addison Avenue, Holland Park, W11 (tel: 0171 603 8267). Old-fashioned, French restaurant that has been in the good food guides for 25 years. Closed Saturday lunchtimes and Sundays.
Clarke's, 124 Kensington Church Street, W8 (tel: 0171 221 9225). Sally Clarke, the chef-owner, offers a no-choice, changing menu and a short choice at lunch. She char grills in the open-plan kitchen and offers Californian, Italian or Japanese dishes. Closed weekends.
Kensington Place, 201 Kensington Church Street, W8 (tel: 0171 727 3184). Noisy, hi-tech, street level, fashionable brasserie with an eclectic menu. Open daily.
Langan's Brasserie, Stratton Street, W1 (tel: 0171 493 6437). Michael Caine's winning

brasserie off Piccadilly, on two floors. Large, noisy and fashionable, with photographers outside ready to snap the inevitable celebrities. Closed Saturday lunchtimes and Sundays.
Leith's, 92 Kensington Park Road, W11 (tel: 0171 229 4481). Recently awarded a Michelin star, Prue Leith's restaurant has one of the best vegetarian menus in London, as well as a choice of two good-value fixed-price menus per night. Closed Saturday lunch, all day Sunday, and Monday lunch.
Simply Nico, 48a Rochester Row, SW1 (tel: 0171 630 8061). A cheaper, simpler version of Chez Nico at Ninety Park Lane (see page 61), with Nico's sous-chef in command, featuring classic and modern dishes. Closed Saturday lunchtimes and Sundays.

For Fish and Oysters
Bentley's, 11–15 Swallow Street, W1 (tel: 0171 734 4756), has an oyster bar, and ex-Ritz chef Keith Stanley creates a range of tempting fish dishes.
Café Fish, 39 Panton Street, SW1 (tel: 0171 930 3999) is a bistro-style restaurant serving good, fresh fish. Reservations are recommended.
Downstairs at One Ninety, 190 Queensgate, SW7 (tel: 0171 581 5666) dishes up a selection of exotic shellfish dishes as well as traditional fish and chips at reasonable prices.

Inexpensive:
There are relatively few good, cheap restaurants in London, but you can often eat cheaply in

FOOD AND DRINK

Indian, Italian and Chinese restaurants (see separate **Ethnic** section).

Otherwise try:

Belgo Centraal, 50 Earlham Street, WC2 (tel: 0171 813 2233). Hip basement café serving mussels, chips and Belgian beer. Expect queues and a bustling atmosphere.

Chapter 11, 47 Hollywood Road, SW10 (tel: 0171 351 1683). Reasonably-priced international dishes are served at this colourful restaurant just off the Fulham Road. The comprehensive wine list is also well-priced.

The Chinoiserie, Hyatt Carlton Tower, Cadogan Place, SW1 (tel: 0171 235 1234). Ground-floor, comfortable, though formal lounge, where snacks and light meals are served from 09.00 to 00.15hrs. A harpist plays at teatime, a pianist during lunch and dinner.

Chinon, 23 Richmond Way, W14 (tel: 0171 602 4082). Tiny French restaurant in a parade of shops in Shepherd's Bush. Excellent value no-choice set menu, though other dishes are pricey. Closed Saturday lunchtimes and Sundays.

The Mountbatten, Monmouth Street, WC2 (tel: 0171 836 4300). Pleasant restaurant in Covent Garden hotel with two fixed-price menus offering interesting English dishes.

Turner's, 87–89 Walton Street, W3 (tel: 0171 584 6711). Good-value French cuisine is provided in this relaxed restaurant where Brian Turner uses quality produce in his creations.

dell' Ugo, 56 Frith Street, W1 (tel: 0171 734 8300). Lively Soho restaurant, bistro and café-bar spanning three floors. Mediterranean and Tuscan fare with daily specials.

Vegetarian

Blah, Blah, Blah, 78 Goldhawk Road, W12 (tel: 0181 746 1337). Tempting menus guaranteed to intrigue even non-vegetarians. Closed Sunday.

Food for Thought, 31 Neal Street, WC2 (tel: 0171 836 0239). Monumental take-aways; some seating. Open daily until 19.45hrs (16.00hrs on Sunday).

Neal's Yard Bakery, 6 Neal's Yard, WC2 (tel: 0171 836 5199). Covent Garden hang-out for serious vegetarians (in among the wholefood shops). Cheap. Open Monday to Saturday, 10.30–16.00hrs.

Govinda's, just off Oxford Street at 9 Soho Street, W1 (tel: 0171 437 4928) is run by the Radhu Krishna sect (but do not worry – there is no attempt to sell their religion) and serves good-value Indian dishes, plus lasagne, pizza, salad and veggie burgers. Cheap. Open noon–20.00hrs Monday to Saturday.

Ethnic

Ethnic restaurants are generally cheap, provided their owners have not inflated their prices just because they have replaced paper tablecloths with linen, lager with wine, and added pot plants. You stand a good chance of getting a table without booking and of finding somewhere open early or late in the evening. Of the thousands of restaurants, a selection is listed below by nationality (with

Get American food at the Hard Rock Café

phone numbers where it is necessary to book).
American: The **Hard Rock Café**, 150 Old Park Lane, W1 (near Hyde Park Corner). Long queues, noisy and cheap. You cannot book. Open daily, 11.30–00.30hrs (01.00hrs Friday and Saturday). **Christopher's**, located in a former Victorian casino at 18 Wellington Street, WC2 (tel: 0171 240 4222) serves American grill-style food including home-made hamburgers, as well as a range of seafood. **Henry J Bean's**, 195 King's Road in Chelsea SW3, (tel: 0171 352 9255) is done out like a 1950s American bar; they serve whisky, cocktails, beer,

burgers and other dishes. For a taste of Mexico and the south, head for Covent Garden's **Café Pacifico**, set in a cavernous converted warehouse at 5 Langley Street, WC2 (tel: 0171 379 7728). Specialities include such dishes as fajitas and chimichanga, washed down by jugs of margerita.
Chinese: London's Chinatown centres around Soho's pedestrianised Gerrard Street. Many restaurants stay open late and although you may have to queue to get in you do not usually have to book a table.
Poons at 27 Lisle Street, WC2 (tel: 0171 437 4549) specialises in wind-dried food. **Harbour City** at 46 Gerrard Street, W1 (tel: 0171 439 7859) is a bustling restaurant in the centre

FOOD AND DRINK

of China Town. There are some 88 varieties of *dim sum* on the menu, together with some of the chef's specialities. For excellent Chinese food, **Ming**, at 35–36 Greek Street, W1 (tel: 0171 734 2721) is the place to go. **Fung Shing**, at 15 Lisle Street (tel: 0171 437 1539) is smarter than most and serves dishes with some interesting combinations and subtle flavours. For insomniacs, **Yung's**, 23 Wardour Street (tel: 0171 437 4986) and **China China**, a new fast-food restaurant at 3 Gerrard Street (tel: 0171 439 7511) both stay open until about 04.00hrs. Outside Chinatown, the best Chinese restaurants are usually more formal and more expensive. One of the first was **Memories of China**, at 67–69 Ebury Street, SW1 (tel: 0171 730 7734), founded by the late Ken Lo who came to London from pre-Revolutionary China. **Ken Lo's Memories of China**, Harbour Yard, Chelsea Harbour, SW10 (tel: 0171 352 4953), has views of boats and a reasonably priced *dim sum* brasserie open throughout the day. There are now numerous branches of the fashionable **Zen** restaurants, all with modern European designer décor: **Zen Chelsea** in Chelsea Cloisters, 85 Sloane Avenue, SW3 (tel: 0171 589 1781) was the first, followed by **Zen W3** (with its cascading waterfall) at 83 Hampstead High Street, NW3 (tel: 0171 794 7863) and **Zen Central** at 20–22 Queen Street, W1 (tel: 0171 629 8089). If you fancy a break from shopping, try the **Good Earth Restaurant**,

The neo-colonial ambience of the Bombay Brasserie

233 Brompton Road, SW3 (tel: 0171 584 3658) where there is a good choice of regional Chinese dishes, while the **Royal China**, 3 Chelverton Road, SW15 (tel: 0181 788 0907) is an up-market restaurant specialising in fish and seafood. **Greek/Cypriot**: The **White Tower** at 1 Percy Street, W1 (tel: 0171 636 8141) is a long-

wine and ouzo), both offering genuine Greek food. Open evenings only, Monday to Saturday. The proprietor sometimes plays the bouzouki. **Indian**: Among the best is the **Red Fort** at 77 Dean Street (tel: 0171 437 2115), expensive but worth it for the unusual dishes that do not feature on more run-of-the-mill Indian restaurants. Equally sophisticated in a decadent colonial sort of way is the palm-strewn **Bombay Brasserie**, opposite Gloucester Road tube station, in Courtfield Close, Courtfield Road, SW7 (tel: 0171 370 4040), with its evening and Sunday lunchtime piano music. **Gopal's of Soho**, at 12 Bateman Street, W1 (tel: 0171 434 0840), is both authentic and inexpensive. Specialities include Goan dishes.

Italian: Leading the fashionable band of Italian restaurants is **Orso**, 27 Wellington Street, Covent Garden, WC2 (tel: 0171 240 5269), a large, fashionable and relatively pricey 1930s-style restaurant (sister of Joe Allen's) with a daily changing menu. Open noon–24.00hrs. **The River Café**, Thames Wharf, Rainville Road, W6 (tel: 0171 381 8824), specialises in traditional farmhouse cooking (open for lunch only on Sunday). In the same rustic vein is the excellent **Osteria Antica Bologna** at 23 Northcote Road, Clapham (tel: 0171 978 4771). Antonio Carluccio's great love of pasta and mushrooms is reflected in the menu at **Neal Street**, 26 Neal Street, WC2 (tel: 0171 836 8368). Other fashionable favourites include

established restaurant serving good Greek and Cypriot food in a warm and friendly atmosphere. There are several restaurants in Charlotte Street, W1, where you can throw plates and dance on the tables, while round the back of Bayswater, in Inverness Mews, there are two neighbouring 20-year-old branches of the taverna-like candelit **Kalamaras**: No 66 (tel: 0171 727 5082 unlicensed) and 76 (tel: 0171 727 9122 – Greek

FOOD AND DRINK

Santini, 29 Ebury Street, SW1, near Victoria (tel: 0171 730 4094), and its elegant younger sister, **L'Incontro** at 87 Pimlico Road, SW1 (tel: 0171 730 6327). **Japanese**: More reasonable than most are **Wagamama**, 4 Streatham Street (off Coptic Street), WC1 (tel: 0171 323 9223), serving large cheap portions and vegetarian dishes. **Yumi**, 110 George Street, W1 (tel: 0171 935 8320), and **Ajimura**, 51–53 Shelton Street, WC2 (tel: 0171 240 0178), an oasis of Japanese calm in the midst of bustling Covent Garden, serve cheap set-price lunches and pre-theatre dinners. Also worth trying is the flamboyant, new **Matsuri**, in the heart of St James's at 15 Bury Street, SW1 (tel: 0171 839 1101), with its popular Sushi bars and Teppan counters. Less expensive is **Miyama**, 38 Clarges Street, W1 (tel: 0171 499 2443) with its good-value set lunch. Also see **Benihana**, Swiss Cottage, under **Where to Eat with Children**, page 104. **Jewish**: **Bloom's**, 90 Whitechapel High Street, E1 (tel: 0171 247 6001), serves chicken soup like mama makes. There is also a branch at 130 Golders Green Road, NW11 (tel: 0181 455 1338). **Lebanese**: **Al Hamra**, 31 Shepherd Market, W1 (tel: 0171 493 1954), offers excellent Middle Eastern food. This fairly formal, busy restaurant (almost opposite the Curzon cinema), has an excellent selection of starters, huge baskets of salads and raw vegetables on every table. Less glamorous is **Maroush I**, 21 Edgware Road,

W2 (tel: 0171 723 0773). The smarter **Maroush II**, 38 Beauchamp Place, SW3 (tel: 0171 581 5434), is near Harrods and is open until 04.30hrs. **Spanish**: London has few Spanish restaurants of note. **Albero & Grana**, Chelsea Cloisters, 89 Sloane Avenue, SE3 (tel: 0171 225 1048) has an attractively decorated restaurant, with a popular *tapas* bar. If you want a genuine smoky *tapas* bar with a guitarist, try the **Mesón Don Felipe**, 53 The Cut, SE1 (tel: 0171 928 3237), which is near the Old Vic theatre. **Thai**: Several of the better Thai restaurants are in Soho. They include: **Bahn Thai**, 21A Frith Street, W1 (tel: 0171 437 8504). **Sri Siam**, 16 Old Compton Street, W1 (tel: 0171 434 3544), and **Chiang Mai**, 48 Frith Street, W1 (tel: 0171 437 7444). The **Blue Elephant**, at the far end of the Fulham Road (4–6 Fulham Broadway), is a fern-filled jungle (tel: 0171 385 6595). By comparison, **Tui**, 19 Exhibition Road, SW7 (tel: 0171 584 8359), is rather plain.

Pubs
People have stopped counting the 10,000-plus pubs in London and lost track of how old some of them are. Needless to say, several of Dickens' and Shakespeare's watering holes are historic enough to be included in sightseeing as well as drinking itineraries.
Do not expect many home comforts in a London pub, but you may get a game of skittles or darts. The food is unlikely to be anything out of the ordinary

either. However, if you want to sample a pork pie, a ploughman's (cheese and bread), bangers (sausages) and mash (potatoes), or shepherd's pie, a pub is the place to do it at a reasonable cost.

New licensing laws mean you can eat or drink all day, though some pubs still shut for a few hours in the afternoon. Closing time is generally 23.00hrs (22.30hrs on Sundays), though a handful of pubs, several down the Old Kent Road (*Tube*: Elephant and Castle), stay open until 02.00hrs. If you want to take children the pub must have a separate eating area. The following pubs are reasonably central or on the river:

Bloomsbury and Holborn
The Lamb, 94 Lamb's Conduit Street, WC1. Small, intimate and friendly pub near Holborn, good for a snack lunch. Small courtyard and original 'snob screens'.

The real test of any pub is the quality of its beer

FOOD AND DRINK

At lunchtime most pubs fill to bursting point

Museum Tavern, 49 Great Russell Street, WC1. Old-fashioned Victorian pub open all day, once frequented by Karl Marx and Virginia Woolf.
Princess Louise, 208 High Holborn, WC1. Popular with Londoners. Rather grand Victorian pub, with lots of polished mahogany. The 'gents' toilet is quiet spectacular.

Chelsea
The Ferret and Firkin, Lots Road, SW10. Jolly pub with basic décor and a singalong piano or guitarist at night.
The Front Page, Old Church Street, SW3. Wealthy Chelsea residents' local. Good food.

Covent Garden
Lamb and Flag, 33 Rose Street, WC2. Low-ceilinged, 18th-century popular pub in an alley. Always packed.

Hampstead

The Holly Bush, Holly Mount, NW3. An 18th-century village pub tucked away in a cobbled courtyard (opposite the station).

Kensington

The Anglesea Arms, Selwood Terrace, South Kensington, SW7. Early Victorian pub. Comfortable and civilized, with a terrace and open fire.

Windsor Castle, 114 Campden Hill Road, W8. Just off the Bayswater Road in Holland Park, an old-fashioned pub with good food and an open terrace garden. Popular in the evenings and at weekends.

Victoria

The Albert, 52 Victoria Street, SW1. Victorian pub frequented by Members of Parliament. Division bell upstairs, huge staircase lined with portraits of Prime Ministers.

The River (including the City and Docklands)

The Anchor, Bankside SE1 (near Southwark Bridge). Dates back to 1750, the third inn on the site, with lots of little rooms and a terrace overlooking the river. Samuel Pepys, the 17th-century diarist, watched the Great Fire of London from here.

The Angel, 101 Bermondsey Wall East, SE16. A 19th-century pub with fantastic views of Tower Bridge from the back gallery overhanging the river.

The Black Friar, 174 Queen Victoria Street, EC4. Arts and crafts décor by Blackfriars Bridge.

Dickens Inn, St Katharine's Way, Docklands, E1. Very popular pub especially at weekends. Overlooks the boats and quayside entertainers, and has an open terrace and exposed wooden beams.

The Dove, 19 Upper Mall, Hammersmith, W6. Cosy, 17th-century riverside pub with tables and chairs outside. Near Ravenscourt Park or Stamford Brook tube.

George Inn, 77 High Street, Southwark, SE1 (near London Bridge Station). The only remaining galleried coaching inn in London, famous during the 18th and 19th centuries and mentioned by Dickens in *Little Dorrit*. Now run by the National Trust. You can sit outside in the cobbled courtyard.

Horniman, Hay's Galleria, SE1. Part of the new modern London Bridge City shopping development. On the Thames with views of HMS *Belfast* and Tower Bridge from the tables outside. Open all day.

Mayflower Inn, 117 Rotherhithe Street, SE16. On the Rotherhithe Walk through the Surrey Docks. The Pilgrim Fathers sailed from here and part of the pub dates back to the 16th century. Weekend barbecues.

Old Thameside, Pickfords Wharf, Clink Street, SE1. New pub between Tower and Blackfriars bridges. Champagne bar and riverside restaurant.

Prospect of Whitby, 57 Wapping Wall, E1. Famous tavern with Tudor beams and flagstones. Live music nightly.

Trafalgar Tavern, Park Row, SE10. Just downriver from the Royal Naval College in Greenwich, atmospheric pub with previews mentioned by Dickens.

SHOPPING

Opening Hours

Most shops are open from 09.00–18.00hrs, with late-night opening until 20.00hrs on Thursdays in the West End and Kensington High Street and on Wednesday in Knightsbridge, King's Road and Sloane Square. Some Bond Street shops are shut all day or half day on Saturdays. Many shops in 'tourist areas' like Covent Garden and Oxford Street are open until 20.00hrs nightly. Sunday opening laws now permit shops to open 10.00–16.00hrs, and tourist areas are covered by by-laws allowing even longer opening hours.

Sales

Prices get slashed at saletime. The winter sales start just before or after Christmas and run until early February. The summer sales begin in June or July and run through August. Look out for the last day of the sales in places like Harrods, where prices are reduced even further. The larger stores have special mid-season sales too.

VAT: See **Money Matters** on page 113 for relief from VAT for overseas visitors.

The Main Shopping Streets and Areas

There are enough shopping areas in London to fill a book on their own. Those below are the main areas.

The West End/Mayfair

Bond Street and South Molton Street
New Bond Street is synonymous with luxury. Once the home of Byron, Nelson and Beau Brummel, Bond Street begins at Oxford Street and runs south towards Piccadilly, becoming **Old Bond Street**, about two-thirds of the way down. Once the most exclusive street in London, it is now more of a mixed bag, though it still offers high quality goods from silver to *haute couture*. Two famous landmarks are Sotheby's the auctioneers (Phillips' is in nearby Blenheim Street), and Asprey's for

exquisite gifts. Fenwicks is good for accessories and women's fashion, while the rather more exclusive White House specialises in linens as well as hand-embroidered clothes for children. You can buy sheet music in Chappell's, shoe shops include Rayne's (suppliers to the Royal family), and you will find exclusive outlets such as Cartier, Hermes, Chanel, Karl Lagerfeld, Ungaro and Ferragamo, and numerous antique shops, silversmiths and fine art galleries.

Pedestrianised **South Molton Street** runs at an angle between Oxford Street and Brook Street, which in turn leads into Bond Street. Here you will find several designer fashion stores; Browns, Katherine Hamnett, Joseph Tricot, Kenzo and Bazaar among them, plus a few

Looking for that special something? Sotheby's might be the place for you

SHOPPING

shoe shops. Café tables spill out on to the pavement in warm weather.

Burlington Arcade, Savile Row and Cork Street

Burlington Arcade, built in 1819, and one of the last bastions of Regency London, runs parallel with Old Bond Street, north of Piccadilly and next to the Royal Academy. It is a covered, glass-domed arcade, lined with quality shops selling everything from antique jewellery to cashmere jumpers and Irish linen. Several are 'by Royal Appointment', and supply the Queen or other Royals. Among the most tempting (running south from Burlington Gardens) are the Irish Linen Company, Christie (who specialise in bronze animals), Hummel (for china dolls and tin soldiers) and Barrett and Co (whose window is full of almost priceless hand-painted miniature chess sets and Russian enamel jewellery). There is a branch of the herbalists Penhaligon's, several jewellers, and Zelli has an exquisite collection of fine porcelain.
If you are interested in art there are a number of galleries, several contemporary, in and around **Cork Street** opposite. Turn left at the end, just past Gidden's of London saddlers, and you are in New Bond Street. Turn right if you want a handmade suit from one of the exclusive tailors in the world-famous **Savile Row**.

Chelsea

The main shopping area of Chelsea is the **King's Road**, which was originally the path

Burlington Arcade

Charles II took to visit Nell Gwyn in Fulham. Livelier than most other fashion areas, there are boutiques of every description, some of them selling whatever is currently in vogue second-hand.

Kensington
A mixed area that includes **Kensington High Street** (department stores and boutiques), **Kensington Church Street** (antique shops), **Portobello Road** antique market, and the tiny, newly fashionable **Brompton Cross**, round the corner from Harrods, with the Conran shop and Joseph's.

Knightsbridge
Knightsbridge is one of the most exclusive shopping areas. Harrods and Harvey Nichols at the top of **Sloane Street** are the two main stores, but you will also find the Scotch House and an Emporio Armani just before you reach **Beauchamp Place**. There are numerous designer boutiques selling fashion and jewellery, and a long line of some of the most stylish designer shops in London leads south down Sloane Street.

Oxford Street
Nearly a mile (2km) long, full of cheap fashion shops and chain stores, interspersed with good-value department stores: Marks & Spencer, Selfridges, C&A, House of Fraser, John Lewis, Debenhams and British Home Stores. Private cars are not allowed in part of Oxford Street, but even the widened pavements have not eased congestion. Illegal marketeers attract crowds that clog up the pavements (and their cheap perfumes will probably be water). Round the back of Selfridges, the pedestrianised **St Christopher's Place** offers quality fashion boutiques and a bit of peace and quiet.

Covent Garden
A fashionable area that attracts young people and visitors. Shops are clustered round the covered central market building, with antiques and crafts sold from the original wrought-iron trading stands. The area can be expensive.

Austin Reed – famous for men's clothes

Piccadilly and St James's

Piccadilly is a busy thoroughfare with airline offices and car showrooms either side of the Ritz and the Royal Academy of Arts. It has old-fashioned shopping arcades (including Burlington Arcade) selling everything from luggage to crystal, Fortnum and Mason, with its exotic food hall, Simpson for clothes and Hatchards for books. Beyond Piccadilly are the indoor shopping complexes of the Trocadero and London Pavilion, while in the

Haymarket, Burberrys sell the famous trenchcoats.

Jermyn Street, south of Piccadilly in St James's, is unashamedly old fashioned and male orientated, offering hand-made shirts and shoes, Havana cigars, antiques, fine art and antique scientific instruments. There is also Floris, perfumiers to the Court of St James since George IV, and half-way along is Fortnum's Fountain Restaurant and a branch of Dunhill's.

Regent Street and Carnaby Street

Regent Street curves down from Oxford Circus to Piccadilly. Designed by John Nash, it houses some impressive buildings including the mock-Tudor façade of Liberty's department store. There are several airline offices, Dickins and Jones department store, a branch of Laura Ashley, Hamleys' toyshop and several shops selling china and crystal, plus the Queen's jewellers, Garrard. Shops specialising in classic British fashion include Jaeger, Austin Reed and Aquascutum. Round the back is the pedestrianised **Carnaby Street**. This used to be *the* street to be seen in during the 1960s, but now it is just a normal shopping street.

Soho

Soho is changing fast but there are still long-established family firms, selling Continental food, coffee, cigars or cakes, though they may soon be pushed out by property developers and high rents as the area becomes even more desirable. The inevitable replacements are boutiques, bars and restaurants. **Gerrard Street** caters for its Chinese community and there is a lively fruit and vegetable market in **Berwick Street**.

Docklands

London's newest shopping centre is the Hay's Galleria, a mall converted from a group of riverside wharves to the east of London Bridge. Here stylish shops and pavement cafés are sheltered by a glass atrium – a hint of what is to come as the whole south side of the Thames is redeveloped.

Tube: London Bridge is the nearest.

Markets

London's market traders are a dying breed as the main wholesale markets get squeezed out of the capital by redevelopment. Covent Garden's fruit and vegetable traders are now in Nine Elms, Billingsgate fish market has moved to West India Dock, and the former Spitalfields' meat market area has shrunk in size as supermarkets now buy direct from farms.

At the turn of the century there were some 60,000 street sellers, called 'costermongers', hawking anything they could get their hands on. The markets of the East End were full of Romany fortune tellers, quack doctors and organ grinders. Food stalls sold pies and eels. You could get your shoes blacked or your knives sharpened. Illegal traders carted off half the food to be sold in poorer districts, talking in rhyming slang (*eg* 'apples and pears'; stairs) to fool the police. Today the street markets that

SHOPPING

are left sell fruit, sometimes of dubious quality unless you know the stallholder, second-hand clothes, and rubbish that has 'fallen off the back of a lorry'. Antiques at largely inflated prices are sold from stalls in Portobello Road, but if you get up early enough there are bargains to be had at the New Caledonian Market on a Friday morning in Bermondsey. As for the old 'costermongers', they are still around in the East End, dressing up in their finest costumes as 'pearly Kings and Queens' for special occasions like the Lord Mayor's Show. The following markets are still going strong:

Antiques
Camden Passage, off Upper Street, Islington, N1 (*Tube:* Angel). Individual stalls on Wednesday (07.00–14.00hrs); Saturday (09.00–15.00hrs), also Thursday for prints and drawings (07.00–16.00hrs), plus quality shops open all week in adjoining streets.
New Caledonian Market, Bermondsey Square, SE1 (*Tube:* London Bridge). Huge open-air market from 05.00 to 13.00hrs on Friday. Trade plus anyone else who gets there early enough. Lots of jewellery.
Portobello Road, W11 (*Tube:* Notting Hill Gate, Ladbroke Grove). The antique-stall holders turn up from 06.00 to 17.00hrs on Saturday. With 1,500 dealers competing for custom, prices can be cut throat. Shops are worth a visit.

Other Goods
Brick Lane, E1 (*Tube:* Aldgate East). East End market. Sunday 06.00–14.00hrs. Lots of rock-bottom rubbish.
Camden Lock, Camden Town, NW1 (*Tube:* Chalk Farm, Camden Town). Several small markets, with crafts and jewellery sold under awnings in the crowded Lock area at weekends (09.00–18.00hrs) when most of the local shops

(prints, furniture etc) are also open. Undergoing redevelopment. Fruit and vegetables are sold in Inverness Street daily, there is a small antique market in Camden High Street on Thursday and at weekends and more bric-à-brac in the **Chalk Farm** market down the road.

Covent Garden, WC2 (*Tube*: Covent Garden). Crafts and mostly British-made goods are sold daily, with antiques on Sunday and Monday. Spills over into the more general Jubilee Market to the south of the piazza (09.00–17.00hrs).

A stall in Camden Passage

SHOPPING

Petticoat Lane. Some stallholders have turned the business of attracting bored shoppers into an art form

Greenwich Market, Greenwich High Road, SE10 (*British Rail*: Greenwich). Weekend market (better on Sunday) selling antiques, crafts and second-hand clothes (09.00–16.00hrs).
Leather Lane, EC1 (*Tube*: Chancery Lane). A bit of everything from cheap silk ties to cassettes, woolly jumpers to palm trees. 140 stalls. Monday to Friday 10.00–14.30hrs).
Petticoat Lane, Middlesex Street, E1 (*Tube*: Aldgate or Aldgate East). Do not look for Petticoat Lane itself because it does not exist. Sunday is the day for clothes. Try Goulston Street at the far end for designer clothes. Brick Lane specialises in electrical goods and furniture. Sunday 09.00–14.00hrs.

ACCOMMODATION

Nearly a quarter of all visitors to London stay with friends or relatives. For the rest the London Tourist Board produces two guides: *Where to Stay in London*, which covers hotels, B & B, guesthouses and apartments, and *London Budget Hotels*. They also have a separate leaflet *Accommodation With Families*. The AA also publishes several guides to London.

The London Tourist Board can book accommodation if you call in at their office at Victoria Station or Heathrow on arrival, or you can write to them at 26 Grosvenor Gardens, London, SW1W 0DU, at least six weeks in advance of your visit. Alternatively, telephone 0171 824 8844. There is a deposit and communication charge when making a reservation (Access or Visa accepted).

Apartments

There are numerous agencies throughout the city that deal with short-let apartments (usually a minimum of one week). You can obtain a list from the London Tourist Board. Agencies include: Apartment Services (tel: 0171 388 3558), Aston's (tel: 0171 370 0737) and Euracom (tel: 0171 436 3201), all offering budget as well as de-luxe accommodation. London's universities open their halls of residence to visitors at Easter and from July to September. Among the most central are the London School of Economics (tel: 0171 955 7575) and John Adams Hall (tel: 0171 387 4086).

Bed and Breakfast

The London Tourist Board lists B & B hotels (see Hotels) as well as agencies that will find you accommodation with a private family. Many of the private homes are in the suburbs and you have no guarantee that you will be included in family life. You may or may not get the option of an evening meal, or a packed lunch, and there may be a minimum stay. Among B & B agencies are:

Central London Accommodation (tel: 0171 602 9668)
Culture Link International (tel: 0171 373 6061)
Host & Guest Service (tel: 0171 731 5340)
London Homestead Services (tel: 0181 949 4455)
Uptown Reservations (tel: 0171 351 3445)
Welcome Assured Limited (tel: 0181 958 3996)
Worldwide Bed and Breakfast Association (tel: 0181 742 9123).

Hotels

London hotels are notoriously expensive although most also offer corporate rates and attractively priced weekend breaks. Some hotels offer free accommodation to children sharing your room and throw in all sorts of extras from rail travel to theatre tickets. Do not hesitate to ask about bargain breaks; even the most exclusive hotels offer them. The following agencies will make hotel reservations for you:

British Hotel Reservation Centre (tel: 0800 282888, toll free)
Hotel Booking Service (tel: 0171 437 5052)
The Leading Hotels of the World

ACCOMMODATION

(tel: 0800 181123, toll free)
Room Centre (UK) (tel: 0171
930 0572).
Hotels recognised by the AA
have met certain criteria and
have been inspected. Given
here is a selection of London
hotels in a variety of locations,
divided up according to price.

Very expensive:
The most exclusive hotels in the
capital are in Piccadilly, Mayfair
and Knightsbridge. The **Ritz** in
Piccadilly (tel: 0171 493 8181)
opened in 1906 and soon
became one of the most
fashionable hotels in the world,
frequented by Royalty and
celebrities from Noël Coward
to the Aga Khan. (The latter had
a suite there for over 40 years.)
If your finances do not run to
staying there you can (if you
book ahead) have tea in the
Palm Court. The sumptuous
Dorchester in Park Lane (tel:
0171 629 8888) is also one of
the world's ultimate luxury
hotels. It has a traditionally
English style and facilities
include a spa and four
restaurants. Equally sumptuous,
with Regency interiors
modelled on Brighton Pavilion,
is the **Lanesborough** (tel: 0171
259 5599) on Hyde Park
Corner. The rather less
flamboyant **Athenaeum** (tel:
0171 499 3464) near Hyde Park
Corner, overlooks Green Park.
The Savoy Group includes the
Savoy, the Connaught,
Claridge's and the Berkeley.
The **Connaught** in Carlos Place,
Mayfair (tel: 0171 499 7070) was
created as a London home for
the landed gentry. The staff
wear morning dress and it feels

*The Connaught Hotel has a country
house feel*

more like a country house than
a hotel. **Claridge's** (tel: 0171
629 8860) in Brook Street
opened its doors in 1899. You
may be welcomed by a
Hungarian quartet. Royalty often
drop in for lunch in the Causerie.

and the American Bar is popular. You will feel quite at home at the **Hyde Park Hotel** (tel: 0171 235 2000) opposite Harvey Nichols in Knightsbridge, where the elegant Edwardian décor feels like a country house. It has wonderful views over the park from the rear.

If you like to work out or have a swim, the **Grosvenor House** (tel: 0171 499 6363) in Park Lane has an attractive indoor pool, as does the **Berkeley** in Wilton Place, Belgravia (tel: 0171 235 6000) where the sliding lid of the rooftop is removed in summer.

Le Meridien Piccadilly (tel: 0171 734 8000) has a Champneys Health Club with a superb Roman-style pool complete with Grecian statues, and the **Hyatt Carlton Tower** in Cadogan Place, off Sloane Street (tel: 0171 235 1234) has a ninth and tenth-floor gym and fitness club, The Peak, which also offers views over Knightsbridge. Overlooking Hyde Park, the **Hotel Inter-Continental London** (tel: 0171 409 3131) and the **Four Seasons** (tel: 0171 499 0888) both cater well for businessmen. The Inter-Continental has a fitness centre and plunge pool. At the Four Seasons the second-floor suites have conservatories. Both hotels have excellent restaurants.

Small Hotels

London's smaller hotels are often converted out of terraced houses, and furnished more like a home. Among the best are: **The Capital** in Basil Street near Harrods (tel: 0171 589 5171); the pretty, chintzy **Halcyon** on the

The **Savoy** (tel: 0171 836 4343) in the Strand recently celebrated its centenary and its standards are still exemplary. At the turn of the century it was so popular with Royalty that the special bell that heralded their arrival was abandoned. There are splendid river views from the highly acclaimed Riverside Restaurant

corner of Holland Park and
Holland Park Avenue, with its
fashionable Kingfisher garden
restaurant (tel: 0171 727 7288);
the ornate **Rembrandt** opposite
the Victoria and Albert Museum
(tel: 0171 589 8100) with a new
Roman-style health club; tiny
22 Jermyn Street in St James's
(tel: 0171 734 2353) where
guests can expect individual
attention and the nearby
Stafford (tel: 0171 493 0111)
dating from the 17th century.
Brown's (tel: 0171 493 6020)
started off small enough when it
opened in 1837, but now
occupies 12 elegant town
houses in Albemarle and Dover
streets off Bond Street, while the
Chesterfield, 35 Charles Street,
Mayfair (tel: 0171 491 2622),
was once the home of the 4th
Earl of Chesterfield.

Expensive enough:
The **Goring**, 15 Beeston Place
(tel: 0171 396 9000), near
Buckingham Palace, has been
going strong since 1910 and is
still owned by the original
family. **The Parkes Hotel**,
43 Beaufort Gardens, SW3 (tel:
0171 581 9944) is essentially a
B & B establishment but
wonderfully central, with
Harrods and Hyde Park just
minutes away. For lovers of
antiques the **Abbey Court** near
Notting Hill High Street (tel:
0171 221 7518) is convenient
for Portobello Road market.
For river views try the modern
Tower Thistle Hotel in
St Katharine's Way (tel: 0171
481 2575), or the slightly more
expensive **Royal Horseguards
Thistle** in Whitehall Court (tel:
0171 839 3400). There are six

Hiltons in London, including the
modern **London Regent's Park
Hilton** (tel: 0171 722 7722) in
St John's Wood, which just
about overlooks Lord's cricket
ground and has a good
Japanese restaurant and New
York deli, and the **London
Mews Hilton** (tel: 0171 493
7222) in Stanhope Row, behind
the **London Hilton on Park
Lane** (tel: 0171 493 8000).

Small Hotels
If you prefer a more personal
atmosphere, the 28-roomed
Beaufort Hotel (B & B and light

One of the bedrooms in Holland Park's Halcyon Hotel

snacks only) in peaceful Beaufort Gardens, near Harrods (tel: 0171 584 5252), is a town house that gives guests their own front-door key. The **Sherlock Holmes** on Baker Street (tel: 0171 486 6161) is full of memorabilia of the great detective and is within easy walking distance of Oxford Street. **Blooms**, 7 Montague Street, near Russell Square (tel: 0171 323 1717) is ideally located for the British Museum. **Five Sumner Place Hotel**, in South Kensington (tel: 0171 584 7586) is part of an impressive Victorian terrace. The rooms are attractively furnished and breakfast and afternoon tea are served in a bright conservatory.

Reasonable:
One of London's best B & B hotels and a winner of awards is the **Claverley** on Beaufort Gardens, a few minutes from Harrods (tel: 0171 589 8541). The **Pembridge Court**, a Victorian town house near

ACCOMMODATION

Portobello Road, in Pembridge Gardens (tel: 0171 229 9977), has only 21 rooms and its own restaurant. Handy for Victoria Station is the friendly **Eccleston Hotel** (tel: 0171 834 8042), and close to Kings Cross Station is the **Holiday Inn** (tel: 0171 833 3900), with spacious bedrooms and good facilities. The **Strand Palace** (tel: 0171 836 8080) occupies a prime location opposite the Savoy. Close to Oxford Street and Marble Arch is the spruce B & B **Bryanston**

Quiet and unobtrusive: the Sandringham Hotel at Hampstead

Court (tel: 0171 262 3141). Reasonably priced for the West End is the **Edward Lear Hotel**, former home of the artist and poet Edward Lear (tel: 0171 402 5401). The hotel is ideally located for both the shops and Hyde Park.

If you do not mind staying in North London, both the **Langorf Hotel**, 20 Frognal (tel: 0171 794 4483), and the **Sandringham** in Holford Road (tel: 0171 435 1569), are near to Hampstead Heath. The West End is a bus ride or a few stops away on the tube, and the areas themselves are worth exploring.

ENTERTAINMENT

There is always an enormous choice of what to see in London, most of it in the West End or just across Waterloo Bridge in the rather ugly concrete South Bank Arts Centre. Opened in 1976, the latter is long overdue for a facelift. Alongside the National Theatre and Hayward Gallery is the Royal Festival Hall, built in 1951 for the Festival of Britain. The neighbouring Queen Elizabeth Hall and the Purcell Room were opened in 1967. The Barbican, in the City, is home to the Royal Shakespeare Company and London Symphony Orchestra, and is a major venue for art exhibitions and concerts. The Royal Opera and Royal Ballet perform at the Royal Opera House, and the English National Opera at the Coliseum.

Dress is fairly informal for concerts and the theatre, but most people dress up for the Royal Opera House. Theatres tend to be hot and stuffy, and although you can leave coats in cloakrooms, queues tend to be long, so a light coat you can fold up and put on your lap is the best idea. In the interval, bars sell drinks (you can order in advance) and light snacks.

Clubs/Discos/Live Music

It is not worth listing what is 'in', because it probably will not be by next week! Needless to say, most clubs are for members only. If you are staying at a top hotel the concierge may be able to get you into a nightclub like **Annabel's** for the evening. If you happen to have media friends in the capital you could

be taken for a drink on a comfortable sofa or a meal at **Groucho's** in Soho. Trendy young Londoners belong to **Fred's** or **Moscow's**. But you have to know a member to get in. If you are from out of town and punk, funk, yuppie or anything else, the best you can do is to buy the weekly *Time Out* magazine and look up the clubs (that do not need membership) currently in vogue. The **Hippodrome**, Charing Cross Road, WC2 (tel: 0171 437 4311) is where to go for a good dance. It is central, loud and expensive, with hi-tech décor and the best lasers in town. **Stringfellow's**, 16 Upper St Martin's Lane, WC2 (tel: 0171 240 5534) is rather more intimate and sophisticated and you can also eat there. Notable live music venues include the **Academy**, 211 Stockwell Road, SW9 (tel: 0171 924 9999); the **Marquee Club**, 105 Charing Cross Road, WC2 (tel: 0171 437 6603); and the **Forum** (formerly the Town and Country Club), 9–17 Highgate Road, NW5 (tel: 0171 284 2200). Eat or drink, listen to live blues, jazz or soul and dance at the **Dover Street Restaurant and Wine Bar**, 8–9 Dover Street, W1 (tel: 0171 629 9813), until 03.00hrs except Sunday.

Jazz

London has few central jazz venues but it does have some informal venues in pubs and restaurants. A selection is listed below.

The Bass Clef, 35 Coronet Street, off Hoxton Square, N1 (tel: 0171 729 2476). Serious venue for young artists who

perform on a stage in a dim
cellar. Cheap food.

The 100 Club, 100 Oxford
Street, W1 (tel: 0171 636 0933).
A small smoky basement which
offers jazz and blues nights with
Caribbean food; also provides
other forms of live music.

Ronnie Scott's, 47 Frith Street,
W1 (tel: 0171 439 0747). In the
heart of Soho, this is London's
most sophisticated jazz club,
dimly lit and smoky, with
regularly changing acts. You
can eat here, but it is expensive.
Booking essential for the most
popular artists. Closed Sunday.
Restaurants with live jazz include:

Pizza Express, 10 Dean Street,
W1 (tel: 0171 437 9595). Jazz
basement.

Pizza on the Park, 11–13
Knightsbridge, SW1 (tel: 0171
235 5550). Near Hyde Park
Corner. Up-market restaurant
with live music every night in
separate basement jazz room.

Concerts/Classical Music

Concerts and classical music
are performed at numerous
venues. If you are in London
during the summer, the **Henry
Wood Promenade Concerts**
(or Proms), held from the end of
July to September in the red-
brick Royal Albert Hall, are great
fun, but queues for the standing
area in the body of the hall can
form early on in the day. The
main classical music venues are:

The Barbican Hall, Silk Street,
EC2 (tel: 0171 638 8891);

Purcell Room, South Bank, SE1
(tel: 0171 960 4242);

Queen Elizabeth Hall, South
Bank, SE1 (tel: 0171 960 4242);

Royal Albert Hall, Kensington
Gore, SW7 (tel: 0171 589 8212);

*The Royal Opera House has been
the setting for many memorable
operatic evenings*

Royal Festival Hall, South Bank,
SE1 (tel: 0171 960 4242);

Wigmore Hall, 36 Wigmore
Street, W1 (tel: 0171 935 2141).
Free concerts take place in the
foyers of the Barbican and the
National Theatre on the South
Bank, at weekends and early in
the evening. Free lunchtime
concerts of organ music, string
quartets, piano recitals, and
brass, many of them in the City.

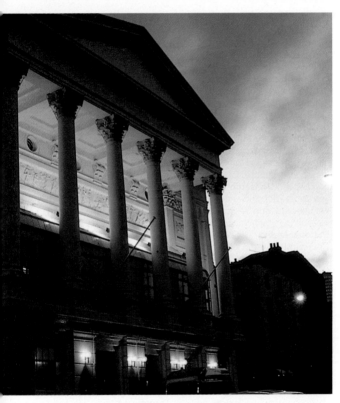

Dance

The Royal Ballet performs at the **Royal Opera House** in Covent Garden. In summer the English National Opera moves out of the **Coliseum** to make room for major ballet companies, while the London Contemporary Dance School as well as touring companies perform at **The Place**. **Sadler's Wells** in Islington is closed until autumn 1998 whilst a new theatre is built, but performances will be held at the **Peacock Theatre** until then. For further details contact:

London Coliseum, St Martin's Lane, WC2 (tel: 0171 632 8300); **Peacock Theatre**, Kingsway, WC2 (tel: 0171 278 8916); **The Place**, 17 Duke's Road, WC1 (tel: 0171 387 0031); **Royal Opera House**, Covent Garden, WC2 (tel: 0171 304 4000).

Opera

The first opera at the **Royal Opera House**, in Covent Garden, was performed in 1817 and they have been playing to packed houses ever since. If you cannot afford a dress circle seat (very expensive) you can always sneak into the famous 'crush bar' during the interval to soak up the atmosphere. The opera house is due to close for renovation work in autumn 1997 and will reopen in autumn 1999. During this time ballet and opera performances will be held at various venues across London. Prices are a lot cheaper and the operas are sung in English at the English National Opera's home at the **Coliseum**. Operas are also performed at other venues including the concert halls on the South Bank. **English National Opera**, The London Coliseum, St Martin's Lane, WC2 (tel: 0171 632 8300). **Royal Opera House**, Covent Garden, WC2 (tel: 0171 304 4000).

Theatre

Most London theatres are in and around Soho and Covent Garden. The **National Theatre** and the **Old Vic** are across Waterloo Bridge on the South Bank, the **Barbican** is in the City. There are also numerous small repertory or 'fringe' theatres all over London. Performances usually begin at 19.30 or 20.00hrs with matinées often on Wednesday and Saturday afternoons. Theatres are closed on Sundays. If your visit coincides with Christmas you will find that many theatres offer a traditional pantomime, while in the summer you can watch a Shakespearean play in the open-air setting of Regent's Park (tel: 0171 486 2431) or in the reconstructed Globe Theatre (tel: 0171 928 6406).

Fringe Theatre: London has an enormous network of fringe theatres extending into the suburbs. Performances are highly regarded, though companies are often ill-funded and perform on a shoe-string. Many take place in pub theatres, some at lunchtime. The most well-known venues include: The **Almeida**, Almeida Street, N1 (tel: 0171 359 4404); **Bush Theatre**, Shepherds Bush Green, W12 (tel: 0181 743 3388); **ICA Theatre**, The Mall, W1 (tel: 0171 930 3647); **King's Head**, 115 Upper Street, N1 (tel: 0171 226 1916); **Riverside Studios**, Crisp Road, W6 (tel: 0181 741 2255).

Be prepared for uncomfortable seats, and minimal scenery. There is no need to dress up. Admission charges are low and you usually have to become a member for a small charge, which you can do at the door.

Tickets

To get tickets for shows and theatre you should use a reputable ticket agency (see **Directory**, page 122). The theatre box offices are usually open from 10.00 to 20.00hrs and you can book over the telephone by credit card or go along in person. You may also be lucky if you queue up for returns on the day. Seats for West End shows are not cheap. The National Theatre is more reasonable. For half-price tickets (to theatres and sometimes for the English National Opera) go in person on the day to the blue and red SWET ticket booth in Leicester Square. There is a small

If you want bargain theatre tickets, the Leicester Square Ticket Booth is the place for you

booking fee, and payment is by cash only. The booth is open from Monday to Saturday from noon until half an hour before the matinée performances and from 14.30 to 18.30hrs for evening performances. Up to four tickets per person only.

What's On

The weekly *Time Out* magazine, and any quality daily, or Sunday, newspaper has details and reviews of what is on. Tourist Offices (see **Directory**, page 122) will also have information.

WEATHER AND WHEN TO GO

Whenever you choose to travel to London, pack an umbrella and a light mackintosh. In the last few years, London's weather seems to have become totally unpredictable. There have been crocuses in bloom in January, the worst storms in memory in October, incessant rain in normally dry June, plus the hottest summer on record.

Traditionally the wettest month is November. July and August are also wet, but the average daily maximum temperatures reach 71°F (22°C). March and April are the driest months, despite what you may have heard about April showers. You may get snow in winter, but you cannot bank on it.

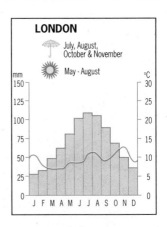

LONDON

July, August, October & November

May - August

To listen to a recorded weather forecast for the London area phone 0891 400101.

Whatever the season, a military band might appear from nowhere to entertain the crowds

HOW TO BE A LOCAL

'Londoners' are hard to define. Cockneys refuse to extend the description to anyone not born within the sound of Bow Bells. North Londoners scoff at South Londoners' claims to be locals, and vice versa. In fact, most Londoners are not really Londoners in any strict sense. It is a diverse, cosmopolitan city – but there are plenty of ways to tell a 'local' from a tourist.

Londoners are always in a hurry. If you feel ignored, do not be offended; they do not talk to each other in public, let alone strangers.

Londoners do not go to the 'historic' pubs on the Thames unless they are next door to the office, and when a publican calls 'time gentlemen please', Londoners have already ordered their last drinks.

Londoners who want to eat their lunch in comparative peace go to the parks; those who are really in the know go to the Inns of Court or to the Temple, where the squares have never emerged into the 20th century. In shops Londoners know better than to expect the assistant to offer much in the way of help and accept that purchases will be scrumpled up and shoved into a plastic bag. They remember to keep the receipt from Marks & Spencer if they think they might need a refund.

Londoners avoid going to supermarkets and West End shops on a Saturday morning. They know that it is much easier to park (and the meters are free) on Saturday afternoon.

They never drive into town without plenty of change for meters and do not expect to get their windscreen washed when they fill up with petrol.

If they go to museums it is with the children in the holidays or on a Sunday afternoon, and they always eat before they go because they know the café will be full and expensive.

Londoners over 30 wait for new films to come round to their local cinema and rarely venture into the West End on a Saturday night except to see a play. They know better than to try to get into a decent film, play or restaurant without booking. Many of the most exciting plays are staged outside the West End anyway, in alternative venues – such as rooms above pubs. Look for these and every other form of entertainment in the weekly magazine *Time Out*.

Londoners hate travelling by public transport. They resign themselves to long waits at bus stops followed by the sudden arrival of a convoy of buses all for the same route.

They know that the tubes will be horribly overcrowded during the rush hour (08.00– 09.30hrs and 16.30–18.30hrs) and they also know that delays are likely at any time. As for the railway network, well it brings many commuters close to tears on a regular basis and that is the only reliable thing about it.

Londoners claim to hate London, but regard anywhere outside the tube line as outer space. They like to describe the city as a series of villages, and enjoy having 'their own' shops and parks, off the beaten track.

HOW TO BE A LOCAL

If Londoners want to go for a walk in the City, they go on Sundays, when the whole of the 'square mile' is virtually deserted. If they want to buy trendy clothes they go to Camden Market and this is also where you can go to see the colourful and eccentric side of London.

Despite their generally grim outlook, Londoners love processions, festivals, marches, demonstrations and anything else that could be described as a 'bit of a do' (it really is true about the use of understatement, by the way).

Derby Day at Epsom. This is one of the great events in the British racing calendar

SPECIAL EVENTS

The London Tourist Board produces a leaflet on events. Some of those that take place on an annual basis are listed below. Exact dates vary from year to year.

January
Lord Mayor of Westminster's New Year's Day Parade.

Marching bands and dancers parade from Westminster Abbey to Berkeley Square, followed by a performance at the Royal Albert Hall.

February
Gun Salute on Accession Day (6th, day after if Sunday); 41-gun salute (noon) opposite the Dorchester Hotel in Hyde Park. Cruft's Dog Show, Earl's Court.

March
The Oxford versus Cambridge University Boat Race, from Putney to Mortlake.

April
Easter Parade (sometimes in March, depending on when Easter falls) in Battersea Park on Easter Sunday, followed by the Horse Harness Parade in the Inner Circle of Regent's Park on Easter Monday.
Gun Salute on the Queen's Birthday (21st).

May
Chelsea Flower Show in the Chelsea Royal Hospital Grounds. Some days open to members only. Apply in advance for tickets.
FA Cup Final, Wembley.

June
Beating the Retreat, Household Division, Horse Guards Parade, SW1. Military display of marching and drilling bands with massed bands and pipers.
Derby Day. Epsom's famous race for three-year-old colts and fillies.
Royal Academy Summer Exhibition, Royal Academy of Arts, Piccadilly (until mid-August).
Stella Artois Tennis

SPECIAL EVENTS

The Regatta always attracts leisurely crowds

Championships, Queen's Club, W14.
Beating the Retreat: Tri-Service Massed Bands, Horse Guards Parade, SW1.
Queen's Official Birthday (Saturday, mid June).
Trooping the Colour. Parade leaves Buckingham Palace at 10.40hrs and travels down The Mall to Horse Guards Parade. Return to Buckingham Palace with flypast by the RAF and appearance on the balcony at 13.00hrs with another gun salute at the Tower of London.
Royal Ascot, Ascot Racecourse, Berkshire. The Queen and the Royal Family attend the famous races. Starts at 14.30hrs each day. Formal attire and a hat essential.
Wimbledon Lawn Tennis Championships, All England Club, Wimbledon, SW19. Late June to early July. Book well ahead for Centre Court tickets.
Henley Royal Regatta, Henley-on-Thames, Oxfordshire. Late

June to early July. International rowing regatta held since 1839.

July

Royal Tournament, Earl's Court, SW5. Spectacular by the Armed Forces in aid of service charities. Attended by the Royal Family.

Henry Wood Promenade concerts, the 'Proms' (informal jazz to symphonic), held at the Royal Albert Hall. Mid-July to mid-September. The last night is the most riotous.

Swan Upping. A traditional ceremony to 'mark' the swans and record their numbers. Takes place on the Thames from Sunbury to Whitchurch (3rd week of July).

August

London Riding Horse Parade, Rotten Row, Hyde Park. A competition to choose the best turned out horse and rider.

Notting Hill Carnival. Held over the Late Summer Holiday weekend in the streets of Notting Hill and Ladbroke Grove. A usually peaceful Caribbean-style procession and party with steel bands, dancing in the streets and lots of loud reggae until 21.00hrs.

September

Horsemen's Sunday. Church service taken by a vicar on horseback at Church of St John and St Michael, Hyde Park Crescent, W2. Horses assemble at 11.30hrs. Ends 13.00hrs then horses go on a procession through Hyde Park.

October

Pearly Harvest Festival Service, held at 15.00hrs at St Martin-in-the-Fields, WC2, attended by London's Pearly Kings and Queens (the traditional cockney costermongers).

Judges' Service. Opening of the legal year on the first weekday in October, with judges in full ceremonial robes. 11.00hrs at Westminster Abbey. View the procession from Westminster Abbey to the Houses of Parliament at 11.45hrs.

Trafalgar Day Parade to celebrate Nelson's victory. Held in Trafalgar Square on the nearest Sunday to the 21st.

November

Guy Fawkes Night (5th). His attempt to blow up Parliament in 1605 is commemorated by bonfires and fireworks on high points in the capital's parks.

London to Brighton Veteran Car Run. Held on the first Sunday in November. Several hundred entrants and their pride and joys in gleaming condition leave Hyde Park Corner early in the morning and take the A23 to Brighton.

Lord Mayor's Show. Takes place on a Saturday in mid-November. The Lord Mayor rides in his gilded coach to the Law Courts for the declaration of office. Colourful floats and military bands start at around 11.00hrs from Gresham Street for Mansion House, passing St Paul's, Fleet Street and the Strand.

State opening of Parliament. Mid-November. The Royal Procession travels along The Mall, through Horse Guards Parade. Departs at 11.00hrs.

Christmas Lights. Switched on in Oxford Street, Regent Street and Bond Street from mid-November until early January.

CHILDREN

There is no accounting for children's tastes. Some like museums, others hate them. The boredom factor may be alleviated by the quiz sheets provided by some of the major museums and galleries, and there are often special events, or films, either at weekends or during the holidays. If you have children who like 'doing things', both the Launch Pad at the Science Museum and the Dinosaur exhibits at the Natural History Museum will provide hours of educationally interactive fun for all ages. Children are charged half-price admission in museums and under 5s usually get in free. There are also numerous other possibilities, from cinemas and theatres that put on children's films and plays, to puppet shows and parks. Babysitters can be arranged via Childminders (tel: 0171 935 2049) or Universal Aunts (tel: 0171 738 8937). One of the most useful sources of up-to-the-minute information is Capital Radio's *London for Kids* magazine (from good bookshops), or the children's section of *Time Out* magazine (available from newsagents). For details of children's clubs, classes, sports and holiday entertainment, call Kidsline (tel: 0171 222 8070), weekdays 09.00–16.00hrs school holidays, 16.00–18.00hrs term time. The following should provide something of interest for most age groups (see pages 25–46 for further details).

- HMS *Belfast*, London Bridge.
- British Museum, Bloomsbury.

Try it yourself – the Science Museum's Launch Pad

- Buckingham Palace (and the Changing of the Guard every morning in summer and alternate mornings in winter at 11.30hrs, also at Horse Guards in Whitehall).
- *Cutty Sark*, Greenwich.
- Geological Museum, South Kensington
- Hampton Court Palace (and the maze), Hampton Court.
- Horniman Museum, Forest Hill.

- London Brass Rubbing Centre, Trafalgar Square.
- London Transport Museum, Covent Garden.
- Madame Tussaud's, Marylebone.
- Museum of the Moving Image, South Bank.
- Natural History Museum, South Kensington.
- Planetarium, Marylebone.
- Rock Circus, Piccadilly.
- Science Museum, South Kensington.
- Thames Barrier, Woolwich.
- Tower of London, City.

Other places of interest for children include:

◆◆
BETHNAL GREEN MUSEUM OF CHILDHOOD
Cambridge Heath Road, E2
A branch of the Victoria and Albert devoted to what man has made for children, with toys through the centuries, dolls and doll's houses, puppets, children's dress and nursery furniture. Saturday workshops

CHILDREN

In the garden of the London Toy and Model Museum

in the art room at 11.00 and 14.00hrs. Holiday activities. Free.
Open: Monday to Thursday and Saturday 10.00–18.00hrs; Sunday 14.30–18.00hrs.
Closed: Friday.
Tube: Bethnal Green (next door)

◆

COMMONWEALTH INSTITUTE
Kensington High Street, W8
Centre for Commonwealth education and culture in Britain. Exhibitions, festivals, workshops and holiday activities. New theme-park style exhibits are planned for opening in 1997.

Open: Monday to Saturday 10.00–17.00hrs; Sunday 14.00–17.00hrs.
Tube: High Street Kensington

◆

DICKENS' HOUSE
48 Doughty Street, near Gray's Inn Road, WC1
A museum since 1925. The house where Dickens lived with his family from 1837 to 1839, and where he wrote his first full-length novel, *The Pickwick Papers*, and later *Oliver Twist* and *Nicholas Nickleby*. Displays include manuscripts, furniture, letters and first editions.
Open: daily, 10.00–17.00hrs.
Tube: Russell Square, Chancery Lane

◆
GEFFRYE MUSEUM
136 Kingsland Road, E2
Collection of period furniture
from 1600 to 1939, and 18th-
century street. Playground in
the garden. Workshops. Free.
Open: Tuesday to Saturday
10.00–17.00hrs; Sundays and
Bank Holidays 14.00–17.00hrs.
Tube: Liverpool Street then bus

◆
HAMLEYS
188–196 Regent Street, W1
Enormous toyshop with six
floors devoted to everything
you can possibly imagine from
dolls and teddy bears to trains
and computers. Soda bar.
Tube: Oxford Circus

◆
LONDON TOY AND MODEL MUSEUM
21–3 Craven Hill, W2
A charming small museum in
two Victorian buildings in
Bayswater with over 3,000 toys
and models dating from the 18th
century to the present day (but
no touching). Trains, boats,
planes and a steam train and
playbus in the garden. Special
events.
Open: Monday to Saturday
10.00–17.30hrs; Sunday and
Bank Holidays 11.00–17.30hrs
Tube: Lancaster Gate,
Paddington, Queensway

◆◆◆
LONDON ZOO
Regent's Park, NW1
The Discover Centre offers an
'animal experience', where
children can put on a helmet
and see how a housefly views
the world, or use a computer
game to 'run like a leopard'.

Also nocturnal creatures,
aquarium, children's enclosure
for close animal encounters,
shows and chats to keepers.
Summer Arklight laser shows
with floats on the canal.
Open: March to September,
daily, 10.00–17.30hrs; October
to February 10.00–15.00hrs.
Tube: Regent's Park, Camden
Town

◆
POLLOCK'S TOY MUSEUM
1 Scala Street, W1 (annexe
opposite and entrance in
Whitfield Street)
Two tiny houses with pint-sized
rooms and narrow staircases.
Founded by the man who made
Victorian toy theatres (for sale
in the adjoining shop and also in
the theatre shop in Covent
Garden). Suitable for small
adults and children.
Open: Monday to Saturday
10.00–17.00hrs.
Closed: Sunday.
Tube: Goodge Street

◆
REGENT'S CANAL
There are a few companies (see
Directory, page 123) offering
boat trips on the peaceful
Regent's Canal between
Camden Lock and Little Venice
(with a stop at London Zoo). At
the Little Venice end, do not
miss the Puppet Theatre Barge
moored in Bloomfield Road,
with captivating performances
at weekends, and daily during
school holidays from November
to May (during June to October
it tours London's waterways; tel:
0171 249 6876 for details).
Tube: Camden for Camden
Lock; Warwick Road for Little
Venice

CHILDREN

Where to Eat

On the whole London restaurants do not take kindly to small children. Some even ban them altogether. You cannot take under-14s into a pub unless it has a separate dining area. Restaurants that do cater well for families include:

Benihana, 100 Avenue Road, Swiss Cottage, NW3 (tel: 0171 586 9508). A Japanese/American restaurant on the ground floor of a modern red and cream building opposite the station. The first in Britain of a US chain offering 'performing' Japanese chefs (juggling pepper pots) on tables for eight, each with its own Hibachi grill. On weekend lunchtimes they have a cheap menu for under-10s (all food grilled in front of them), plus crayons and a Punch and Judy show (Sundays) in the bar. Not so cheap for grown-ups.

Smollensky's Balloon, 1 Dover Street, W1 (tel: 0171 491 1199). Opposite the Ritz. Noisy basement, with weekend lunchtime fun (children's half-hour show at 14.30hrs) includes balloons, children's menus, a resident clown and a magician, plus videos, story time and Punch and Judy upstairs. Food is mostly steaks.

Smollensky's Balloon is one of the places that welcomes children

TGI Friday's, 6 Bedford Street, WC2 (tel: 0171 379 0585). Another American-style restaurant that makes a fuss of children, especially at lunch on Sunday (face-painting and magician). Vegetarian dishes and 'build your own burgers'.

Entertainment

Barbican Centre, Silk Street, EC2 (tel: 0171 638 8891). Exhibitions, workshops, concerts (free) and Saturday and holiday cinema club.
Tube: Moorgate, Barbican

ICA Children's Cinema, Nash House, The Mall, SW1 (tel: 0171 930 3647). Regular Saturday and holiday film shows.

Tube: Charing Cross, Piccadilly Circus

The Little Angel Marionette Theatre, 14 Dagmar Passage, off Cross Street, N1 (tel: 0171 226 1787). Weekend and holiday puppet shows.
Tube: Highbury and Islington

National Film Theatre, South Bank, Waterloo, SE1 (tel: 0171 928 3232). Weekend matinées of films. Also arts workshops at the National Theatre, Royal Festival Hall and Hayward Gallery (tel: 0171 921 0848).
Tube: Waterloo

Polka Children's Theatre, 240 The Broadway, Wimbledon, SW19 (tel: 0181 543 4888). Some way from central London but one of the best children's theatres in the capital with regular plays for all ages, and also workshops. Puppets and playground. Closed Sundays and Mondays.
Tube: Wimbledon, South Wimbledon

Puppet Theatre Barge, Little Venice, Bloomfield Road, W9 (tel: 0171 249 6876). String puppet show on a moored Thames barge in Maida Vale.
Tube: Warwick Avenue

Tricycle Theatre, 269 Kilburn High Road, NW6 (tel: 0171 328 1000). Children's shows Saturday 11.30 and 14.00hrs.
Tube: Kilburn

Unicorn Theatre for Children, 6 Great Newport Street, WC2 (tel: 0171 836 3334). The only solely professional children's theatre in the West End. Plays for all ages. *Performances*: 13.30hrs Tuesday to Friday, 14.30hrs weekends and during school holidays.
Tube: Leicester Square

TIGHT BUDGET

Accommodation
● The Youth Hostels
Association, 14 Southampton
Street, WC2, near Covent
Garden (tel: 0171 836 1036) will
help you find cheap
accommodation.
● As an alternative, the London
Tourist Board will direct you to
bed and breakfast hotels.

Eating and Drinking
● Pubs with decent food are
generally a lot cheaper than
restaurants of whatever sort.
● Wine bars have reasonably
priced food but the wine is
expensive.
● The cheapest meals of all are
to be found in cafés (sausage,
bacon and egg, washed down
by a cup of tea).
● You can get a cheapish meal
at any number of restaurants
serving pizzas.
● Indian and Chinese
restaurants can also be cheap
provided you steer clear of the
new wave of 'designer'
restaurants in and around Soho
and Covent Garden.

● A cheap alternative to lunch is
to buy a sandwich from any one
of numerous sandwich bars.
● If you are prepared to start
your evening off early, you can
get half-price cocktails at bars
that offer a Happy Hour.

Entertainment
● If you cannot afford a full-
price ticket to a West End
theatre, go to the SWET
ticket booth in Leicester Square
for half-price tickets on the day.
● Cheaper still are the tickets
for pub or fringe theatres.
● National Theatre seats are
cheaper than the West End.
● Free concerts are held in the
National Theatre foyer, at the
Barbican, in churches and in the
piazza at Covent Garden.
● Several of London's museums
are free, including the British
Museum, though most expect
some sort of donation (see
What to See section).
● Some museums and galleries
offer a reduction if you have got
a student card.

St James's Park is free entertainment

Contents

DIRECTORY

Airports

Useful phone numbers:
Gatwick Flight Enquiries, tel:
0891 757757
Heathrow, tel: 0891 757757
London City Airport, tel: 0171
474 5555
Luton, tel: 01582 405100
Stansted, tel: 01279 680500

● **Gatwick**. To the south.
Regular British Rail trains (every
15 mins, or hourly before
06.20hrs) leave from within the
terminal and run into Victoria
Station in 30–45 minutes.

● **Heathrow**. To the west. You
can get to and from central
London by Underground,
Airbus or taxi (very expensive).
The **Airbus** runs from all four
terminals to Victoria or Euston,
stopping at several points
including major hotel areas *en
route*. The journey takes
between 50 and 85 minutes,
with services every 20 or 30
minutes. Airbuses are
equipped with wheelchair lifts
and secure accommodation. At
Victoria and Euston there are
Carelink wheelchair-accessible
bus services linking most of the

central London main-line railway
stations. You buy tickets
(reasonably cheap) on the bus.
Unless you are staying right in
the centre of London this is the
most relaxing bet, especially if
you have heavy luggage,
although it takes a bit longer
than the tube.
The **Piccadilly Underground**
line runs from Terminals 1, 2 and
3 with a separate stop for
Terminal 4. Trains depart from
central London every 4–7½
minutes on average. Allow about
45 minutes to reach Piccadilly
Circus. At Acton Town the
Piccadilly line joins the main
Underground network and you
can change trains at appropriate
stations to reach all parts of
central London. If you have got
heavy luggage you will have to
struggle up stairs and escalators.
A **Night Bus** service between
Heathrow and Trafalgar Square
(Route N97) operates nightly at
about hourly intervals. Tickets
bought onboard.
You can buy **Heathrow Transfer
Tickets** in advance through
overseas travel agents or in
London hotels, Travel Information
Centres and travel agents.

UNDERGROUND

UNDERGROUND

Travel Information 0171-222-1234
Travelcheck 0171-222-1200

© London Regional Transport

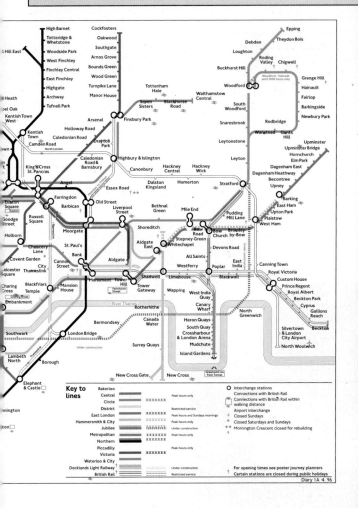

• **London City Airport**. This small airport caters mainly for business travellers hopping between European capitals. It is located in the Dockland, 6 miles (9.5km) east of the Bank of England and the City. The Green Line 787 service runs from Victoria Station to the airport or trains run to Silvertown British Rail Station (less than a quarter of a mile from the airport) via West Ham or Stratford on the Central or District lines respectively. Allow at least half an hour for the journey. Taxis are also available at the airport.

Car clamping is very effective – and very annoying

• **Luton**. British Rail have a combined rail and coach link between St Pancras and the airport via Luton Station. The journey takes about 45 minutes. Trains from King's Cross Thameslink are more frequent.
• **Stansted**. Direct British Rail train services to Liverpool Street Station every 30 minutes. The journey takes 45 minutes. Trains also stop at Tottenham Hale Station where there is direct access to the Underground's Victoria line.

Camping
Sites include:
Hackney Camping, Millfields Road, E5 (tel: 0181 985 7656). Four miles (6.5km) from the centre. Open mid-June to August.
Abbey Wood Caravan Club, Federation Road, SE2 (tel: 0181 310 2233). Good access into central London; open all year with first-class facilities.
Tent City, Old Oak Common Road, W3 (tel: 0181 743 5708). As central as you can get (near East Acton tube). Open June to September.

Chemists see Pharmacies

Crime
It is best not to travel alone on the Underground at night. Keep bags and wallets safe, especially in crowded places. Otherwise London is much the same as other capitals.

Driving
Londoners are not bad drivers. One-way streets and trying to park legally are the main problems. There are special 'bus and taxi only' lanes that operate during peak hours in the

West End and yellow 'boxes' in which you are not supposed to stop across junctions. Traffic in central London tends to snarl up during the 'rush hours' from 08.00 to 10.00hrs and from 17.00 to 19.00hrs, and also when theatres close at around 22.30hrs. Seat belts are compulsory.

Car Breakdown. If you are not a member of a motoring organisation you can join on the spot. The AA is Britain's largest motoring organisation; for breakdown assistance, telephone freephone 0800 887766.

Car De-clamping. London has four different car pounds and payment centres where you must go if your car has been clamped in central London – so follow the instructions given on the label attached to the vehicle. Alternatively, the Car Clamp Recovery Club (tel: 0171 235 9901) will, for a fee, do it for you.

Car Hire. Agencies include:
Avis, tel: 0645 123456
Budget, tel: 0800 626063
Eurodollar, tel: 01895 256565
Europcar, tel: 0171 834 8484
Express, tel: 0171 801 0077
Hertz, tel: 0345 555888
London Car Rentals, tel: 0171 486 4141
Payless, tel: 0171 584 3260
Thrifty, tel: 0500 070000 (toll free)
Chauffeur-driven Cars.
Avis, tel: 0171 917 6703
Barclay Cars, tel: 0171 878 7099
Brunswick Chauffeur Car Services, tel: 0171 727 2611
Location Chauffeurs, tel: 0171 629 1555
London Limousine, tel: 0171 928 9280

Securicor Chauffeur Drive, tel: 0171 498 5995

Parking. Car-parks (numerous National Car Park – NCP – parks) cost a little more than meters. One of the most central is the vast NCP car park beneath Marble Arch, entered by means of the northbound carrigeway of Park Lane. Other central car parks are at Cambridge Circus, W1, and Brewer Street, W1. Most meters in central London are blue and only take £1 coins. You are not allowed to 'feed' your meter when it has run out of time, but can use time already clocked up. Parking in some areas is free after lunchtime on Saturdays and all meters are free on Sundays. Traffic wardens are dressed in yellow and black. You cannot park in a resident's parking bay (unless you have got a permit), on a double yellow line (at any time) or on a single yellow line during working hours (usually including Saturday). Check the signs on lamp-posts to see exactly what the rules are. An illegally parked car may get clamped or towed away to a Police Pound and you have to pay a fine to get it back (see **Car De-clamping**). If you cannot find your car, ask a policeman.

Petrol. Most petrol stations are self-service and some stay open 24 hours a day. Unlike their counterparts on the Continent you cannot expect to have your windscreen washed. If you need assistance you must call the breakdown services (see **Car Breakdown** above) or go to a garage with a mechanic. Most repair garages shut at weekends.

Electricity
240 volt, 50 cycle AC. Shavers
operate on 240 or 110 volts.
Plugs are three-prong.

Embassies and Consulates
Virtually every country is
represented. Addresses are
listed in the Yellow Pages
phone book under 'embassies',
or ask at the London Tourist
Board.

Emergency Telephone
Numbers
Dial 999 from any telephone,
give the location, and state
whether you want Fire, Police
or Ambulance (which will take
you to the nearest hospital).

Entertainment (see page 89).
For what's on, see weekly
events listings in *Time Out,* the
Evening Standard or in the
quality Sunday papers.

Hospitals
There are **24-hour casualty
departments** at: University
College Hospital, Gower Street,
WC1 (tel: 0171 387 9300);
Guy's Hospital, St Thomas
Street, SE1 (tel: 0171 955 5000);
St Bartholomew's Hospital, West
Smithfield, EC1 (tel: 0171 601
8888).
Moorfields Eye Hospital is
situated at City Road, EC1 (tel:
0171 253 3411).
Private emergency treatment
is available from Medical
Express, 117a Harley Street,
W1 (tel: 0171 499 1991),
Monday to Saturday only.

Lost Property
Go to the nearest police station
to report any loss.
If you have left something on a

Familiar red buses in Oxford Street

bus or tube the London
Transport Lost Property Office
(tel: 0171 486 2496) is at 200
Baker Street, NW1 (*open*:
Monday to Friday 09.30–
14.00hrs). For losses on trains
ring the arrival/departure point
of the train you were travelling
on. If you have left something in
a taxi try to remember its licence
number (not number plate) and
telephone 0171 833 0996.

Money Matters

Banks (see **Opening Times**).
The terminals at Gatwick and
Heathrow have 24-hour banks.
Currency. When banks are
shut you can change money at
major travel agencies like
Thomas Cook, in the exchange
offices at major department
stores or in the numerous
bureaux de change in high
streets and at stations. Look for
agencies that indicate that they
follow the BTA Code of Conduct
if you do not want to be
cheated. There are exchange
facilities at National Girobanks
at some large post offices in
central London.

VAT (Value Added Tax) is added
to most goods and services at a
standard rate of 17½ per cent.
You can get relief from VAT on
goods (*eg* shopping) but not
services (*eg* restaurants) if you
are a visitor from abroad. You
may have to spend a minimum
amount (usually over £100).

Opening Times

Banks. Monday to Friday
09.30–15.30 or 16.30hrs. Also
Saturday mornings (09.30–
12.00hrs) at some branches.
Business. Normal business
hours are 09.00 or 10.00–17.30
or 18.00hrs. Offices are shut at
weekends.
Museums and Galleries. Most
are shut Christmas Day, Boxing
Day and New Year's Day,
others on all public holidays
and on Sunday mornings. Some
museums and galleries are
open shorter hours during the
winter months.
Pubs. They are allowed to open
Monday to Saturday 11.00–
23.00hrs, Sundays and Bank
Holidays from 12.00–15.00hrs
and again from 19.00–22.30hrs.
Not all pubs choose to stay
open in the afternoon.
Shops. Most shops open at
09.00 or 09.30hrs and shut at
17.30hrs. Shops open until

*Chelsea Harbour, base for a
waterborne commuter service*

19.00 or 20.00hrs on Thursdays in the West End and on Wednesdays in Knightsbridge and Chelsea. They are often open late daily in Covent Garden and Oxford Street. Some shops open on Sundays.

Pharmacies

There are pharmacies all over London. Bliss, 5 Marble Arch, W1; Boots, 75 Queensway, W2 and 254 Earls Court Road, SW5 are pharmacies which open late.

Places of Worship

Practically every religion is represented somewhere in London. See Places of Worship, in the Yellow Pages directory.

Public Holidays

New Year's Day, Good Friday, Easter Monday, May Day (first Monday in May), Spring Bank Holiday (last Monday in May), Late Summer Holiday (last Monday in August), Christmas Day, Boxing Day.

Public Transport

● **Buses**. From the upper deck of one of London's double-decker buses there is often a good view of the capital. Three million passengers a day use the buses. Bus stops show bus numbers and timetables, but make sure you ring the bell or put your hand out at a red 'request' stop. There are 41 miles (66km) of bus lanes in central London, so while the rest of the traffic stands still, buses (and taxis) keep moving. 'Pay-as-you-enter' night buses all stop at Trafalgar Square.

● **Coaches**. Victoria Coach Station is the main London terminal for longer distance express coaches. Information from National Express Coaches (tel: 0171 730 0202). London Transport run coach tours in and around London and to places of interest near by, with a courtesy pick-up service from hotels. Most leave from Wilton Road Coach Station, near Victoria Station (tel: 0171 823 6567). Green Line coaches connect central London with the suburbs. The main terminal is at Eccleston Bridge near Victoria Station (tel: 0181 668 7261).

● **Disabled**. London Regional Transport run a special unit to help disabled passengers, including braille maps for the visually impaired. For free advice on the easiest and cheapest way to travel in and around London, Tripscope (tel: 0181 994 9294) provides an excellent service. Airbus services between Heathrow and central London have been converted to accept wheelchairs. At Victoria and Euston the Carelink wheelchair-accessible bus service links main-line stations. There are also Mobility Buses with wheelchair access on routes in and around London, and the Docklands Light Railway can accommodate wheelchairs. Details from London Regional Transport, Unit for Disabled Passengers, 55 Broadway, SW1 (tel: 0171 918 3312).

● **Docklands Light Railway (DLR)**. The Docklands Light Railway, built to cater for the redevelopment of the Docklands, opened in 1987. The toy-town-like, blue and red, driverless trains run on weekdays only (until 21.30hrs), departing from Bank Underground station

DIRECTORY

The tube stations are gradually being re-vamped

and Tower Gateway (take the Underground to Tower Hill) via Shadwell through the Isle of Dogs to Island Gardens (walk to and from Greenwich through the Greenwich foot tunnel under the Thames). Trains also run between Island Gardens and Stratford, connecting with the Underground and British Rail. An extension east to Beckton in the Royal Docks is due to open shortly.

British Rail Travel Centres (for personal visitors) are at: 14 Kingsgate Parade, Victoria Street, SW1; 407 Oxford Street, W1; and 87 King William Street, EC4. Telephone enquiries: 0171 928 5100 (24-hour service).
Docklands Light Railway (tel: 0171 918 4000).
London Transport 24-hour Telephone Information Service gives you the choice of recorded information or speaking to an operator: 0171 222 1234 or 0171 222 1200.

London Regional Transport, 55 Broadway, SW1H 0BD (tel: 0171 222 1234).
London Transport (LT) Information centres can be found at the following stations: Piccadilly Circus, Oxford Circus, King's Cross, Euston, Victoria and at Heathrow Central at Terminals 1, 2 and 3, and in all the arrival halls. They also sell tickets for excursions.

• **Minicabs**. Minicabs have acquired a bad name because of the touts that cruise the streets looking for gullible passengers who they then trick by charging outrageous fares. In fact, it is illegal for them to tout and you should never trust yourself to an unknown driver, who is likely to be uninsured, not to mention the risks of getting robbed or worse. However, there are some perfectly respectable and well-established companies whose rates (especially over long distances) are often cheaper than the black-cab fares. Reputable services include:
Atllas Cars (tel: 0171 602 1234)
Embassy Cars (tel: 0181 200 1111)
Lady Cabs (run by women for women, tel: 0171 272 3019).

• **Taxis**. London taxicabs are black or maroon with a white licence plate at the back. You can hail them when the yellow taxi sign on the roof is alight. There are ranks outside mainline stations and major hotels. A taxi can be ordered by telephoning 0171 286 0286, 0171 253 5000, 0171 272 0272 or 0171 727 7200. A tip of between 10 and 15 per cent is expected. Taxi drivers are a mine of information. The driver must use his meter (within the Metropolitan District). There is a minimum charge shown on the clock, and supplements for luggage, after 20.00hrs and at weekends.

• **Tickets**. The **Visitor Travelcard** is available to overseas visitors, for 1, 3, 4 or 7 days and must be bought abroad. It offers virtually unlimited travel on the tube and buses (as well as discount vouchers to top attractions) and saves money on the regular

DIRECTORY

Travelcard available once you get here. It can be bought from travel agents and London Transport sales agents abroad (you do not need a photo).

Heathrow Transfer Tickets (see **Airports**, page 107).

The regular **Travelcards** are available from any Underground station. They give freedom to travel on the buses or Underground for 1 or 7 days, or a month, within selected zones. You need a passport-sized photo for a 7-day or monthly card. Journeys for one-day cards have to start after 09.30hrs and are restricted between 16.30 and 18.30hrs (Monday to Friday) but you can travel any time at weekends. You can also get a bus pass (for a day, week or month) though it is not available for the central London zone.

Underground or Tube Tickets. Single or return tickets must be bought at the station before you begin your journey. They must be kept to show an inspector who might board the train, and to operate the exit barriers at the other end. Expect to be treated as a fare-dodger if you buy the wrong ticket.

On **buses** you pay the conductor if there is one or the driver (as you board) if there is not. Keep your ticket until you leave the bus in case an inspector gets on. London is divided up into six **zones** for fare purposes. Travel within central London is one zone. See maps at stations for details. **Children** under 5 travel free. Under 14s get reduced rates (up to a third off the price), while 14 and 15-year-olds must carry a child-rate photocard (available from post offices and travel information centres with a photo and proof of age) for their reduction.

● **Trains**. British Rail trains terminate in central London at various stations. Each station serves a network of stations in certain directions, as indicated below.

Moorgate, King's Cross (Yorkshire, North East and East Coast to Scotland); tel: 0171 278 2477.

Euston, Marylebone, St Pancras (Midlands, North Wales, North West and West Coast to Scotland); tel: 0171 387 7070.

Paddington (West of England and South Wales); tel: 0171 262 6767.

Blackfriars, Cannon Street, Charing Cross, Fenchurch Street, Holborn Viaduct, Liverpool Street, London Bridge, Victoria and Waterloo (East Anglia and Essex, South East and South); tel: 0171 928 5100.

● **Underground**. The London Underground (or Tube) runs deep under the capital. Two and a half million people travel on it daily. There are 273 stations; those in central London are within a few minutes' walk of each other. You should not have to wait long for a train, but they can get uncomfortably crowded during the rush hour (roughly between 08.00 and 09.30hrs and 17.00 and 18.30hrs).

The Underground is divided into lines: Bakerloo, Central, Circle, District, East London, Jubilee, Metropolitan, Northern (which has one of the longest continuous railway tunnels in the

Many London pubs now stay open all day long

world), Piccadilly and Victoria. Maps are easy to follow with each line having a different colour (see pages 108–9). The lines criss-cross making it easy to switch from one line to another although at some stations this can mean long walks down (well-lit) corridors or several rides on escalators.

Some stations have numerous platforms: Baker Street has ten. The destination will be marked on the front of the train and also on a board above the platform. Some lines branch into two so check the destination carefully. Most stations have automatic barriers which open when you insert a ticket. All the main-line stations have connections with the Underground.
It is not permitted to smoke

anywhere on the Underground. The Underground shuts at night with last trains leaving central London stations at midnight or soon after (an hour earlier on Sundays). First trains at 05.30hrs (07.00hrs Sunday).

Senior Citizens

Senior citizens or OAPs get reduced entry into many museums and galleries. There are also reductions for women over 60 and men over 65 on public transport on production of a Senior Citizen Railcard (UK residents), or a Rail Europe Senior Card or a BritRail Pass (overseas visitors).

Sport

Sportsline (tel: 0171 222 8000) provides information on what is on where. The *Time Out Guide to Sport, Health and Fitness in London*, from bookshops and newsagents, lists venues. For the major sporting events like Ascot, Wimbledon or Henley you will need to book tickets well in advance through a ticket agency such as First Call (tel: 0171 497 9977).

Student and Youth Travel

London can seem like a pretty cruel city if you are a student. Essential reading is *Time Out*'s free *Student Guide,* produced in conjunction with the NUS (National Union of Students), particularly if you are planning to stay for a while. Hang around the NUS in Malet Street, WC1, to meet fellow students.
An International Student Identity Card is essential if you want discounts in museums, galleries, theatres, cinemas and on public transport. The main

student organisations in London are: Student Travel Association (STA Travel), 74 and 86 Old Brompton Road, SW7 (tel: 0171 937 9962 Intercontinental, 0171 937 9921 European).
University of London Union, Malet Street, WC1 (tel: 0171 580 9551). See also **Tight Budget** (page 106).

Westminster Abbey is one of the great treasures of London

Telephone and Postal Services

Post Offices generally open Monday to Friday 09.00–17.30hrs; Saturdays 09.00–12.00hrs. The post office behind Trafalgar Square in King William IV Street, WC2, is open Monday to Saturday 08.00–20.00hrs. Stamps (only of certain values) are also available from machines outside some post offices, or as books of stamps in newsagents etc. The old red phone boxes have now almost all been replaced by open glass booths. You can use a phonecard in some of them (available from post offices or newsagents). If you are out of cash call the operator (dial 100) to reverse charges/call collect. For calls within London, you need only use the prefix 0171 (inner London), or 0181 (outer London), if calling across the

0171/0181 boundary (check the number of the telephone you are calling on), otherwise simply dial the number. International numbers start with 00. Push-button phones take coins which you insert after you have lifted the receiver but before you dial.
Useful numbers include:
Directory Enquiries (London) 142
Directory Enquiries (UK) 192
International Directory Enquiries 153
International Call Collect 155
Emergency 999

Ticket Agencies

It is cheaper to book direct, but agencies may have tickets for sold-out events, at a price. Agencies will take credit card bookings over the phone. They include:
First Call, tel: 0171 497 9977
Keith Prowse, tel: 0171 631 4604
Ticketmaster, tel: 0171 344 4444
Wembley Box Office, tel: 0181 900 1234

Time

British Summer Time (BST) begins in late March when the clocks are put forward one hour. In late October the clocks go back an hour to Greenwich Mean Time (GMT). The official date is announced in the daily newspapers and is always on a Saturday night. Just remember March forward and Fall back!

Tipping

Taxi drivers expect 10 to 15 per cent of the fare. Most restaurants include service in their bill, but even so some leave the total amount on credit card slips blank. Some ethnic restaurants do not include service. Doormen at hotels expect £1 for getting taxis etc. Porters at railway stations expect £1 (standard charge of £5 at Heathrow Airport).

Toilets

There are some sanitised booths in the centre of London, otherwise there are coin-operated public toilets in main-line stations and free toilets in most large stores. All parks have toilets, as do many squares.

Tourist Offices

The **London Tourist Board** operates Tourist Information Centres at:
Victoria Station Forecourt, SW1. Open Easter to end October, daily, 08.00–19.00hrs; November to Easter, Monday to Saturday 08.00–19.00hrs; Sunday 08.00–16.00hrs. This is the main information centre for London and it can handle hotel, theatre and transport bookings (though you may have to join a long queue for these) and give general advice. There is also a shop selling a comprehensive range of maps, guides and souvenirs. Branches of the London Tourist Board, with opening hours, are as follows: Selfridges, Oxford Street, W1 (Basement). Open store hours. Heathrow Terminals 1, 2, 3, Underground Station Concourse. Open daily, 08.00–18.00hrs. Liverpool Street Underground Station. Open Monday 08.15–19.00hrs; Tuesday to Saturday 08.15–18.00hrs; Sunday 08.30–16.45hrs. The **London Tourist Board** is not geared up for telephone enquiries, but does offer a

Part of Buckingham Palace's Changing of the Guard – a 'must' for many visitors

large number of pre-recorded information lines (see phone books for the complete list) including one that gives details of the week's events and highlights (tel: 0891 505440). The best general enquiry telephone service is the Capital Helpline on 0171 388 7575.

For travel outside London:
Northern Ireland Tourist Board, tel: 0171 355 5040
Scottish Tourist Board, tel: 0171 930 8661
Wales Tourist Board, tel: 0171 409 0969
There are also regional tourist offices throughout Britain.

Tours of London
If you want a guided tour of the capital there are numerous possibilities.
● **By Boat**. The Regent's Canal runs from Camden Lock to the Zoo and Little Venice (Maida Vale): a quiet backwater with a towpath you can walk along. Companies include:
Jason's Trip (tel: 0171 286 3428). They use gaily painted narrow boats and trips last 1½ hours. Easter to early October. Refreshments and commentary

on board. Also lunch and dinner cruises. Boats leave from opposite 60 Bloomfield Road in Little Venice, W9.

Jenny Wren Cruises (tel: 0171 485 4433). Leave from Camden Lock. They are based at 250 Camden High Street on the bridge over the canal. Sunday lunchtime cruises run all year.

London Waterbus Company (tel: 0171 482 2550). Runs daily, on the hour, from Camden Lock to Little Venice from April to September (weekends only rest of year, every 90 minutes). Also day-long trips through East London to Limehouse and the Docklands.

The Thames. Covered cruise boats ply the river. Most boats have snack bars on board with informal commentaries (in English only). They depart from the following piers:

Richmond (tel: 0181 892 0741) to Hampton Court and a circular cruise to Teddington Lock.

Westminster (tel: 0171 930 4721) down river to the Tower, the Thames Barrier and Greenwich (all year); up river to Kew, Richmond and Hampton Court (summer only). Also circular cruises and evening and lunch cruises.

Charing Cross (tel: 0171 839 3572) to the Tower and Greenwich; also evening cruises.

Tower (tel: 0171 488 0344) up river to Westminster and down river to Butler's Wharf and Greenwich (all year) with a ferry to see HMS *Belfast*.

Greenwich (tel: 0181 858 3996) to the Tower, Charing Cross, Westminster and down river to the Thames Barrier. Also lunch cruises every Sunday.

General riverboat information (tel: 0891 505471).

● **By Bus**. London Transport run 1½-hour sightseeing tours by double-decker bus (open-topped in summer), with a commentary by a qualified guide. They start from Marble Arch, Victoria, Piccadilly and Baker Street, and French and German speaking guides are also available. There are sightseeing buses to the Zoo (March to early September) from Oxford Circus and Baker Street stations.

● **By Coach**. Numerous companies offer coach tours of London as well as excursions to nearby places of interest. Tours run by Evans and Evans (tel: 0181 332 2222) are led by London Tourist Board qualified guides.

● **On Foot**. Guided walks usually start at Underground stations. Some follow a theme – Cockney London, the Jewish East End and Jack the Ripper among them. Companies include: Citisights (tel: 0181 806 4325), Tour Guides International (tel: 0171 495 5504), Historical Tours (tel: 0181 668 4019), The Original London Walks (tel: 0171 624 3978) and Tours by Tape (with a guidebook, in several languages) are available from the Tourist Information Centre bookshop at Victoria Station.

One of the most relaxing ways to see London is to take a boat trip. The view below is looking upstream from Tower Bridge. The Chelsea Pensioner (right) spends his time at the Royal Hospital. The hospital was founded in 1682 for veteran soldiers

ACKNOWLEDGEMENTS

Acknowledgements
The Automobile Association would like to thank the following
photographers, libraries and hotels for their assistance in the
compilation of this book:

AA PHOTO LIBRARY 34 *Cutty Sark* (R Surman), 82 Petticoat Lane
(S & O Mathews).

SUSAN GROSSMAN 36 Freud Museum, 88 Sandringham Hotel,
104/5 Smollensky's Balloon.

HALCYON HOTEL 86/7.

NATURE PHOTOGRAPHERS LTD 46 Red deer stag (C B Carver)
49 Ancient oaks (F V Blackburn), 50 Purple hairstreak, 52 Green
sandpiper, 53 Yellow rattle, 55 Grazing marsh, 56/7 Epping Forest,
59 Water rail (P R Sterry).

POWERSTOCK PHOTO LIBRARY Cover Big Ben.

RITZ HOTEL 64.

BARRY SMITH was commissioned to take all the remaining photographs,
and these are held in the Association's own library (© AA PHOTO
LIBRARY).

Author's Acknowledgement:
Susan Grossman thanks the London Tourist Board for their help in
preparing this book.

Contributors for this revision:
Verifier: Christopher Catling; Copy editor: Sheila Hawkins